The Voluntary Principle

Other Books by the Same Author:

Embattled Wall

Protestant-Catholic Marriage

The Ecumenical Mirage

The Great Church-State Fraud

Co-Author:

The Churches: Their Riches, Revenues, and
Immunities

Praise the Lord for Tax Exemption

The Religious Empire

THE

VOLUNTARY

PRINCIPLE

C. Stanley Lowell

Joseph J. Binns, Publisher
Washington—New York

Library of Congress Catalog Card Number 77-87235
ISBN 0-88331-093-7

Contents

Preface

This will acknowledge my debt to Andrew Leigh Gunn, executive director of Americans United for Separation of Church and State, and Elvin Benton, director of the Department of Religious Liberty of Columbia Union Conference of Seventh-day Adventists, for a critical reading of the manuscript and helpful suggestions. Also, to Glenn L. Archer, president of the Americans United Research Foundation, for his advice and counsel, and, to Doris Black for her invaluable assistance in preparing the manuscript. I am grateful, too, for the sponsorship of *The Voluntary Principle* by the Americans United Research Foundation through the action of its Board of Directors.

Having made these acknowledgements, let me hasten to state that the ideas expressed in the book are my own responsibility. In the hope that they may kindle a smoldering fire into blaze, they are hereby offered to all who believe in the effective power of religion.

1. Voluntary Religion

One of the most observable of human traits is that of grudging reluctance in the performance of required duties, however essential, as contrasted with pleased alacrity in voluntary pursuits. The nature of the performance can be quite irrelevant. A birdwatcher will sit for hours in the utmost discomfort because he is doing something that pleases him, something he has decided is fun. A sentence to attend a rock and roll concert would be regarded by many as an ultimate exercise in cruel and unusual punishment. Yet thousands assemble in unspeakable discomfort for such events and count them as pleasure. What we want to do is fun; what we don't want to do is drudgery. The former is attractive and pleasant; the latter, however essential it may be, is disagreeable and at best a bore.

The art of government would, therefore, seem to lie in lending attraction and appeal to those performances which are basic to human survival. Men should be enticingly appealed to rather than preemptorily commanded. We should manage, if at all possible, so that men will rejoice to do the right and regard the wrong as painful burden. The trouble with this is that in most cases it does not seem to work. What is essential and beneficial gets a bad name while what is banal and dangerous somehow assumes the glitter of attraction.

A basic task confronting society is that of appealing to its own constituency. It is the task of attracting its members to the kind of performance necessary to survival, making that performance exciting and appealing. Immediately we think of this as the function of government. Why? Because we have grown accustomed to think of government as handling everything. It is government that launches programs in the grand manner, pours out vast expenditures, gets things done.

Yet with all its resources and its might, it has become obvious that government is failing to provide the social dynamic so sorely needed. Public officials themselves frequently exhibit the most tawdry behavior, accepting bribes for official favors, covering up the sordid record of their own misdeeds. There is a fundamental reason for this failure quite beyond the sinful nature of individual persons. It is the fact that government is constantly concerned with coercion, is built up on coercion, and coercion is never very inspiring. However prosaic, governments are definitely necessary. Some forms of virtue are required for survival and governments are constructed to mandate them.

Anything beyond the survival level (i.e., beyond the level of coercion) is beyond the effective scope of government. Here we move into an area where people cannot really be coerced in their performance but will produce or not according to their own desire. A man can be compelled by law to refrain from robbing banks and compelled by law to pay his taxes, but the same kind of compulsion cannot require him to discover a cure for cancer, paint a picutre or give his life for another. Here we enter an entirely different area where people can be challenged and appealed to but never compelled.

At this point we are no longer involved with compulsion but with volition. This is uniquely the realm of religion. Here we have to reckon with that strange power which has motivated the saints and inspired the martyrs who joyfully laid down their lives for their beliefs. The reformers—Luther, Calvin, Zwingli, Huss and Knox—were men possessed by convictions that propelled them. They were not menials putting in an eight-hour day with fringe benefits. They were gladly dedicating their abilities and their very lives to a cause dearer than all else. It was a labor of love and much more; it was the kindling power of religious inspiration working its wonders.

Consider, further, the pioneer spirits whose vision and drive have illumined the Christian movement. Theirs was a spiritual thrust with few parallels. Men like David Livingston, Adoniram Judson and David Brainerd exhibited a zeal hardly comprehensible to the non-religious. These men were the counterparts of St.

Paul in another age. They were imbued by a power and impelled by it to total dedication. It drove them on to achievements which seemed to range beyond the realm of the possible.

It is evident that when we encounter such spirits as these we have left compulsion far behind. This is not the realm of the obligatory but of the voluntary where men rejoice to go beyond what any legal compulsion could require of them. It is here that we find the glory and grandeur of life.

We see voluntaryism at work, again, in the great religious revivals of history. Religious revivals at their best have featured a kind of spiritual contagion, a kindling from soul to soul, which proved almost irresistible to those it touched. Converts suddenly became willing and eager to undergo rigorous discipline and to donate their effort and money to the cause that enchanted them. They were willing to go the second mile and more in dedicated service. Sacrifice was welcomed; labor cheerfully volunteered. What would have been the crassest kind of regimentation if required by law became joyful privilege for the believer.

A classic example of spiritual contagion is to be seen in the Protestant Sunday School movement of the 1800's and early 1900's. It was a product of the great American revival. While it often included the clergy, just as often it did not—kindling its evangelical fervor quite apart from the church's professional leadership. It reached Americans of all races and classes and denominational affiliations. Other movements in society such as the civil rights crusade or the movement for world peace could not compare with it in either fervor or durability. A few years and the latter were done while the Sunday School rolled with powerful momentum for more than a century and survives in some quarters to the present day.

The Sunday School lasted till the professionals took it over. Eventually, its program became regularized and organized under professional direction. With the coming of religious education directors the Sunday School lost its luster and went into the decline which still continues.

The Great Awakening of the 18th century and the missionary movement of the 19th and 20th centuries were impressive examples of voluntaryism at work. The religious services conducted by such diverse leaders as Jonathan Edwards and George Whitefield resulted in numerous conversions wherein persons happily surrendered their evil ways and habits in order to pursue a new way of life. Likewise the missionary call was heeded by many who dedicated their lives henceforth to proclaiming the Christian message in remote lands.

Another offshoot of the great American revival was the denominational college. A passion for knowledge was sparked by the passion for God. Baptist, Methodist, Presbyterian, Congregational, Lutheran and many other religious groups established and maintained a host of institutions of higher learning. Many of these were, and are, institutions of excellence. Here again, however, the distinctive emphasis has been blunted and largely lost. As

13

government began to assume substantial financial responsibility for these schools, their spiritual fervor cooled. Tax funds from the public sector were bound to have a chilling effect on the spiritual thrust of such institutions.

It was the genius of the Founding Fathers to recognize that religion operates in one realm, government in another. Voluntaryism was integral to religion whereas government relied on coercion. The two were not antagonistic; it was just that their processes could not effectively interlock. Churches were basically agencies which relied not on coercion but on voluntary response. To mingle their affairs with those of government was not practicable. What the Founders wanted to do about religion was basically to loose it and let it go—to let it be and do what it would so long as it did not impair the rights and liberties of the people.

It was the conscious goal of the Founding Fathers to seek minimal government, leaving the individual with all possible freedom. A creature of dignity and worth, man was to be left free to develop save for those restraints recognized to be socially necessary. Nowhere did the Founders exhibit their wisdom more clearly than in their relegation of religion to the voluntary realm. There was to be no "official religion." There was to be no state promotion of any particular religion or of religion in general. The churches were to be on their own, subject to rise or fall at the will of their adherents.

Religion would receive only one thing from the state—an opportunity—"free exercise," it was called. The churches were to have complete freedom to do

14

whatever they wished—provided it did not transgress civil law or interfere with the rights of others. They were free to win adherents, solicit contributions, purchase property, erect buildings, even to engage in unrelated commercial business. All the churches received from the arrangement was freedom, but freedom was everything.

The rationale for this arrangement lies deep in the realities of human nature. Religion sparks heavy overtones of emotion and, indeed, it ministers to the emotional life of man. This explains why wars of religion are invariably the bloodiest of all conflicts. Men will fight determinedly for trade concessions or poltical status, but they will battle to the death and beyond for the correct doctrine of the procession of the Holy Spirit. The emotional overtones of such issues are all but incredible. Yet history repeatedly bears witness to their force. The only comparable phenomenon is a war pitting brother against brother. Here, again, emotional involvement is very great and, as our own Civil War demonstrated, can result in the most sanguinary of conflicts.

To implement these emotional commitments with political force impressed the Founders as a highly inflammatory procedure. Instead of stating legal requirements in the realm of religion, why not handle its explosive potential with a policy of benign neglect? Why not just give it freedom to rise or fall and let it alone?

So Zelotes Fuller observed:

"The past history of the Christian Church

should be a solemn warning to us never to permit an alliance to be formed between the priesthood and the civil magistry—between church and state powers."[1]

The Founders understood that religion cannot be coerced by the state because it is inherently voluntary. Attempts to interrelate religion with the political (coercive) process are literally self-defeating. That is the negative aspect of the church-state issue. On the positive side we should note the tremendous contribution religion can make to human well-being in its purely voluntary role. What because of its very nature cannot be coerced can be voluntarily embraced with the most extraordinary results. Moses, Jeremiah, Isaiah, Amos, St. Paul, St. Augustine, Luther, Calvin, Zwingli, Knox, Bunyan, Wesley—there is an endless roster of ordinary men who, touched by the burning flame of religion, became great. No legislature can effectively pass laws which require religious performance. No executive decree can mandate them. But religion's challenge to the conscience of man can and frequently does produce phenomenal results.

This is not all. It is religion that has produced not only the fire for the phenomenal but the sustaining strength for the ordinary. Society readily falls into chaos without the faithful cohorts of little people who from somewhere derive the strength and will to perform its drab daily tasks. If they fail, all fails. If they effectively persist, even the most stupid leadership at the top is hardly enough to insure failure. The great contribution of religion lies at just this point—its ability to inspire people in the kind of performance that is necessary for human survival. Religion is capable of putting a policeman in every heart, thus obviating the need for one on every corner. The difference between abdication and dedication is often provided by religion. This is its preeminent role. Religion remains the classic expression of the voluntary principle in human behavior.

This is by no means a complete definition of religion. It takes no account of theology. It makes no mention of religion as a discipline or as a field of knowledge to be mastered—like mathematics or chemistry. It deals with religion only pragmatically—in terms of its significance for human behavior. Even its doughty foes acknowledge that it has wielded enormous influence at this point. To be sure, religion has sometimes impelled men to forms of behavior that have been stupid and tragic. But it has also inspired some of the noblest moments of recorded history. The potential for good is enormous. Religion can make men want to be good and do good. As such, it is the most important force in the world.

Footnotes

1.   Joseph L. Blau, *Cornerstones of Religious Freedom in America*, 1949.

2.   Religion and the State

The religious enterprise has always played a leading role in the shaping of culture. In fact, religion has usually been, along with political rule, a dominant force. It follows that the relation between church and state is of immense significance to both and to the people. The Council of Nicea in 325 A.D. is a convenient point from which to date the commencement of an intimacy between church and state hitherto unknown to Christianity. It was the Emperor Constantine who summoned the bishops to Nicea, made all arrangements for their entertainment and presided at the sessions. It was the emperor who, with the clergy's consent, brought state and church into a working alliance, each supportive of the other. This was a change in the status and role of the church that was fraught with profound consequences. There is every reason to describe the Council of Nicea as one of the decisive happenings of history.

How the union of church and state was spurred by Nicea and developments shortly thereafter is quickly demonstrated. At Nicea, Christianity became the officially established faith of the empire. A series of decrees gave the clergy tax exemption and immunity from military service. The wealth of any dying without direct heirs accrued to the church. Only Christians were eligible for high posts of government. Construction and repair of churches was financed from public funds. All properties of the pagan cults were turned over to the Catholic Church. Clergy stipends were provided from tax funds. All pagan cults and dissident Christian sects were banned; their properties were confiscated and turned over to the Catholic Church. Heretics were slaughtered or driven into exile. There was complete church-state union between the Catholic Church and the Roman Empire.

The shift of civil authority from opposition and persecution of Christianity to acceptance and sponsorship was not so drastic as might at first appear. The civil power is always concerned, first and foremost, with its own survival. There is some justification for this. The civil power is nothing if it cannot effectively rule. If it cannot maintain its authority it must step aside, or more likely, be brushed aside by a succeeding regime. Successful political authorities are concerned with every threat to their rule. It is part of their management responsibility to beware of any new movement which might conceivably jeopardize their own power and prestige. Once the new Christian movement got off the ground and began to attract a following, the civil authorities would tend to become apprehensive. Eventually, they sought to eliminate its threat to their own prerogatives by oppression and persecution.

There was, however, an alternative: join forces with the rising movement. Use it as a bulwark of the establishment, making such concessions as might be necessary for the purpose. This was the kind of arrangement envisaged and initiated by the Emperor Constantine. What it eventually came to mean was that the civil power would grant the church official status, tax exemption for its property, public subsidy for its clergy and institutions and elimination of all heretical or rival sects. On its part, the church pledged political support to the emperor and his regime.

At precisely that moment the glory of the Christian movement ended and its days of ignominy began. The church had forsaken its voluntary character and chose to rely on the state's coercion. From that time forward the story of the church becomes increasingly doleful. The fact that it survived at all may not be due to its divine nature, as its apologists proclaim, but rather to the momentum supplied by its superb start in the first three centuries. As a volunteer movement winning men by the sheer power of its attraction, the church had built a firm foundation which even the infamous arrangements commencing in 325 A.D. and the consequent rot, were never quite able to destroy.

Another redeeming virtue of the church was a kind of inner vitality which enabled it to proliferate into voluntary sects and thus preserve its cutting edge. There was also the Protestant Reformation of the 16th century which erupted as a voluntary movement with sufficient strength to effect a permanent rift in the Roman religio-political monolith. Sad to relate, however, the Protestant movement which began with great promise soon allied itself with the civil power as the Roman Church had done earlier. The unholy alliance ended the prophetic power which Protestanism had originally demonstrated as voluntary, reforming sects. Official establishment drained and stunted the Protestant churches just as it had the Roman Church twelve centuries earlier.

The effect of such a church-state detente is ruinous to the church. It makes the religious life merely a phase of one's civil duty. One is a "good Christian" just as he is a "good citizen." The religious becomes immersed in the civil. The religious tax is levied like any other tax. State and church are intertwined and all but identical. Under this arrangement the church has security but very little else. Certainly there is no dedication, no commitment, no prophetic excitement. So far as the individual is concerned, it is the difference between doing what he wants to do and loves to do and doing what he has to do. The form and trappings remain; the glory is gone.

The basic reason for the loss to religion in this transition is the shift from volition to compulsion. As we have seen, law must finally rest upon compulsion. But to inject this concept into religion is totally inappropriate. To compel a man to be religious is a contradiction in terms. Without freedom at this point, his religion is a sham and a farce. A religion that is not free is not a religion. It is something else—a state-mandated performance.

A kind of church-state compact remains in some areas as the concordat—a vestigial survival of medievalism. It is almost grotesque to see church and state continue to enter into political partnership involving joint commitments to each other. The entire theory is wrong: volition and coercion cannot effectively mix. What is really involved in all such endeavors is a shift by the church from voluntaryism to a reliance on compulsion.

A concordat is not the only way this disastrous shift can come about. We see in our time a process of the state's buying into the church by means of public subsidies. An affluent government appears willing to finance with tax funds practically any private endeavor whose directors are able to bring pressure to bear upon it. Churches have all too readily fallen into this practice. We see this development in church housing, welfare, health and education programs. It has been estimated that churches and their institutions in the United States receive about $4.5 billion annually in subsidies from federal, state and local governments.[1] These subsidies are for church programs in the following categories: hospital construction and health services, education in elementary secondary and higher categories, the Economic Opportunity Act, housing and urban development, surplus commodities and property, research and development. All these forms of aid are at the federal level. States and municipalities have also provided aid in various categories for church institutions.

It can, of course, be argued that the church programs are good and that they provide useful services to the people. There is some truth in this. But the other side of the coin is what happens to the ministry of the church in this kind of arrangement. The spiritual concerns of the church fade. They are subsumed in the more generalized concerns of the state. Indeed, the religious subsidy may be described as the 20th century method of emasculating the church of its prophetic role. The broad concern of "public good" quickly permeates the tax-subsidized service or institution. The religious thrust fades. It works this way: first, a little money with a little regulation. Then, more money with complete control. So the church is drawn to the self-destruction which partnership with the state always seems to bring.

To give but one graphic instance of this: consider the case of federal aid to sectarian colleges. There is a specific provision set by the Supreme Court as a necessary condition of such aid that buildings erected with federal funds on the campuses may never be used for religious worship or religious instruction. That is spelling out specifically what is bound to happen to any church institution receiving the state's funds. The purpose of its founding must be ignored and forgotten. Even if this were not spelled out in the specifics of the law, it would have such a practical consequence.

A dramatic example of what happens can be seen

in the case of Western Maryland College, once an institution of the United Methodist Church. In exchange for financial aid from the state government the school agreed to remove all religious symbols and indicia from the campus and its buildings, declassify itself as a Methodist institution, become completely neutral as to religion, neither sponsor nor conduct religious services, not finance any religious organization or receive financial aid from any, not elect more than 10 percent Methodists to the Board of Trustees and formally disassociate itself from the United Methodist Church.

Money has to be an important concern for the churches. In at least this respect churches are like other institutions—they need money to survive. The practice of supporting the church by taxes had an age old rationale. The church was basic to the moral structure on which the state must depend. Without this structure the state itself could not exist. Therefore, public subsidies for the church were readily justified and, indeed, were the all but universal practice.

Voluntary religion was something new. It was based on the idea that people might want religion, freely choose it, freely love it, and freely contribute for its support. But what if nobody bothered? What if religion were to languish for lack of funds and lack of popular interest? Then it would just have to disappear and die. Said Benjamin Franklin with his earthy wisdom:

"When religion is good, I conceive it will

25

support itself; and when it does not support itself, and when God does not take care to support it so that its professors are obliged to call for help of the civil power, 'tis a sign, I apprehend, of its being a bad one."[2]

Some of the Founding Fathers understood this kind of separation of church and state perfectly and stressed both the unwisdom and the futility of trying to mingle the two. We see this clearly in Thomas Jefferson's famous letter to the Danbury Baptists:

"Believing with you that religion is a matter which lies solely between man and his God, that he owes account to none other for his faith or his worship, that the legislative powers of government reach actions only, and not opinions, I contemplate with sovereign reverence that act of the whole American people which declared that their legislature should 'make no law respecting an establishment of religion, or prohibiting the free exercise thereof,' thus building a wall of separation between Church and State."[3]

The place of religion as quite beyond the orbit of the state's coercion is clearly depicted by Jefferson in his draft of the Virginia Bill for Establishing Religious Freedom in 1786.

"We, the General Assembly of Virginia, do enact that no man shall be compelled to frequent or support any religious worship, place, or ministry whatsoever, nor shall be enforced, restrained, molested, or burthened in his body or goods, or shall otherwise suffer, on account of his religious opinions or belief; but that all men shall be free to profess, and by argument to maintain, their opinions in matters of religion, and that the same shall in no wise diminish, enlarge, or affect their civil capacities.[4]

The importance and desirability of severing religion altogether from the state's coercive processes was made explicit by James Madison in his *Memorial and Remonstrance.*

"Because experience witnesseth that ecclesiastical establishments, instead of maintaining the purity and efficacy of Religion, have had a contrary operation. During almost fifteen centuries, has the legal establishment of Christianity been on trial. What have been its fruits? More or less in all places, pride and indolence in the Clergy; ignorance and servility in the laity; in both, superstition, bigotry, and persecution."[5]

Madison's rhetorical question on this point has echoed around the world:

"Who does not see that the same authority which can establish Christianity in exclusion of all other religions may establish, with the same ease, any particular sect of Christians in exclusion of all other sects? that the same authority which can force

27

a citizen to contribute threepence only of his property for the support of any one establishment may force him to conform to any other establishment in all cases whatsoever?"[6]

It has often been said that religion and politics do not mix. This simplistic saying gropes for a profound truth. The two are not irrelevant or antagonistic. They simply move in different orbits. The civil government is indispensable since it provides society with a context of order. But the greatness and glory of life flow from voluntary decisions where men do what they freely choose to do. It is in this realm that religion operates.

The civil order has sometimes been hostile to the man of religion. This was certainly true of Christianity in its early days. It was only after three centuries of a resplendent prophetic ministry that Christian leaders consented to establishment of their faith with the tragic results we have noted. Enemies of the church could do no better than to work for its official establishment— and generous state subsidies. That would nicely do it in as history so clearly teaches.

Organized religion is undergoing serious reverses in our time. Both Protestant and Roman Catholic churches alike have suffered. There has been a steady decline in church attendance over the past decade. According to the Jesuit magazine *America*, attendance at Catholic mass declined from 71 percent to 55 percent between 1958 and 1973. This despite the compulsory rule which remains in effect. The decline in youth attendance is now accompanied by a decline in attendance of the middle-aged. Vocations for the priesthood have declined throughout the world. Over the past decade 13,450 priests, world-wide, have left their ministry. Catholic nuns who once supplied free teaching service in parochial schools now provide but a third of these staffs. At the same time many thousands of Catholic parents, disillusioned with Catholic schools, are withdrawing their children from these institutions and enrolling them in public schools. The *Catholic Directory of 1972* reported that in the preceding year 580 Catholic schools closed their doors and that the number of children in Catholic elementary and secondary schools had declined by 361,910. By the end of 1975 Catholic schools had lost nearly half the enrollment they had recorded a decade earlier.

Three thousand Protestant ministers are said to leave the ministry each year. The United Methodists, once this nation's largest Protestant body, have been losing members at the rate of 100,000 to 200,000 a year. In the 12 year period through 1976 the Methodists lost 1.2 million members. The United Presbyterian Church has declined more slowly but just as surely. Since 1966 its membership has registered losses of 10,000 to 105,000 each year. Because of a decline in donations the denomination's national staff has been reduced by 25 per cent. The overseas missionary force has been cut from 1,000 to 500. The Lutheran bodies in North America registered a decline in membership of 62,429 during the years 1970 and 1971. The Episcopal Church has reported a steady decline in membership since 1969.

Membership in the United Church of Christ

declined from 2,067,223 to 1,895,016 between 1964 and 1973—a drop of 8.3 per cent. While the denomination's gifts increased during the period, as United Church of Christ President Robert Moss pointed out, the increase was not enough to keep up with inflation.

The circulation of church magazines registered a profound slump in the 1970's. The United Methodist *Together* lost a staggering 150,000 in circulation and folded. *Presbyterian Life* dropped 95,000 and the *American Baptist Magazine* lost 75,000. Alfred Klausler, the executive director of the Associated Church Press, summed it up: "The main denominations are not holding their own."

Is there any connection between the religious slump and the growing dependence of the church on the state? Certainly the two developments are taking place at the same time. And we have certainly learned that official establishment and subsidy have never revitalized the religious enterprise. Rather the reverse.

The reason for this is easy to detect. When the subsidy enters the church institution, some other things enter with it. Government regulation and control come in and this is only proper as care must be taken to see that the funds are spent for the intended purpose. It would be unthinkable to give precedence to a particular creed or to deny enrollment or leadership in the institution on the basis of creedal tests. In a free country public subsidies must be administered equitably and without sectarian bias even when they go to a religious institution. Thus, the life line of the church institution is severed. Its distinctive element is shattered and eliminated. It becomes merely another public institution serving a public purpose.

Our leaders have long recognized the impotence of civil authority in matters of religion. Said Justice Douglas in his dissent in *McGowan v. Maryland*: "If religious leaven is to be worked into the affairs of our people, it is to be done by individuals and groups, not by government."[7]

Justice Clark was right when he recalled in *Abington v. Schempp* that "the place of religion in our society is an exalted one, achieved through a long tradition of reliance on the home, the church, and the inviolable citadel of the individual heart and mind."[8]

So President Ulysses S. Grant: "Leave the matter of religion to the family, the altar, the church and the private schools, supported by private contributions. Keep the church and the state forever separated."[9]

One of the most eloquent admonitions on the issue of state-mandated religion as opposed to voluntary religion is contained in a message from James Madison penned in July 1812:

"If the public homage of a people can ever be worthy of the favorable regard of the Holy and Omniscient Being to whom it is addressed, it must be that in which those who join in it are guided only by their free choice, by the impulse of their hearts and the dictates of their consciences; and such a spectacle must be interesting to all Christian nations as proving that religion, that gift of Heaven for the good man, freed from all coercive edicts, from that unhallowed connection with the powers of this world which corrupts religion into an instrument or an usurper of the policy of state, and making no appeal but to reason, to the heart, and to the conscience, can spread its benign influence everywhere and can attract to the divine altar those freewill offerings of humble supplication, thanksgiving, and praise which can alone be acceptable to Him whom no hypocrisy can deceive and no forced sacrifices propitiate."[10]

There is a virility about voluntary religion. It is quite capable of reaching and kindling the minds of the people. But when the state becomes involved, an atrophy sets in which nullifies its splendid potential. The best thing the state can do for religion, therefore, is to let it alone.

Footnotes

1. Larson, Martin A. and Lowell, C. Stanley, *The Religious Empire,* 1976. Chapter 20.
2. *We Hold These Truths*, compiled by C. Stanley Lowell and Albert J. Menendez, 1974.
3. Stokes, Anson Phelps, *Church and State in the United States*, Vol. I, 1950, p. 335.
4. *Ibid.*, Vol. I, p. 302.
5. *Ibid.*, Vol. I, p. 341.
6. *Ibid.*, Vol. I, p. 341.
7. *McGowan v. Maryland*, 336 U.S. 420, 1961.
8. *Abington v. Schempp*, 374 U.S. 203, 1963.

9. Address delivered in Des Moines, Iowa, Sept. 29, 1875.
10. Brant, Irving, *The Bill of Rights: Its Origins and Meaning*, 1965, p. 418-419.

3. Voluntaryism at Work

We are contending here that the decisive area of human achievement is to be found not where men are coerced but where they freely respond—not where they are compelled but where they volunteer. From the depths of volition rise the decisive achievements of mankind.

This is by no means to derrogate coercion. Society could not exist without it. Vast populations existing in intricate social contexts must be impelled and restrained according to necessary norms or they could scarcely survive. We are restrained from appropriating our neighbor's property and goods and required to respect law and order. We are directed to stop on the red and go on the green. Many times each day we are confronted with imperatives of the law which direct and circumscribe our behavior in ways necessary to our complicated existence.

The more crowded the planet becomes the more

need for coercion and regimentation. When a man's nearest neighbor lived miles away, that was one thing. But when the population is packed jowel to jowel and piled one upon another in lofty towers—that is something else. All the logistics of crowded propinquity cry for controls. Thus, the role of legal coercion is bound to grow. All of this, however, is as dull as it is necessary. There is said to be a sublime majesty about the law. In theory this may be true, but it is not so in local practice.

What man cries out in exultation at the thought of paying his taxes? Who leaps for joy at the approach of the April 15 deadline? All recognize the necessity of taxes but none rejoice in their payment. What normal boy races with burning eagerness to his school each day? Education is compulsory. School is a place he has to go. In his more reasonable moments he may acknowledge the desirability of it, but of glowing fondness there is likely none.

In a country which separates church and state the effect is to free religion from the burden and handicap of the state's coercion. Under such an arrangement religion is completely removed from the realm of coercion and becomes strictly voluntary. People embrace it only if they really want to. There are many advantages and even protections for religion under this plan.

It has been said that one cannot go ten miles in any direction in the United States without encountering a church. Every church is there for the same reason— some folks wanted it to be there. They got together, contributed the funds to buy the land and raise the walls. No government bureau was involved. The people did it themselves. They wanted to do it and they did it.

The ban on tax funds for the support of religion contains a built-in protection against anti-clericalism. Anti-clerical eruptions have almost always been occasioned by state establishment and sponsorship of religion. What happens is that under the preferred treatment of the state the church becomes too rich and too powerful politically. Getting much, it uses what it has as a lever to get more. The church in such a situtation frequently ends up owning most of the best land—all tax-exempt—and enjoying vast emoluments and extensive political power. These benefits wrought at the expense of the people are certain to arouse their resentment and the end result is revolution and expropriation. We have seen this drama enacted with almost monotonous consistency in many lands: in Germany, France, England, Scandinavia, Russia, the Philippines, Mexico—to name a few. These upheavals were really not directed against religion as such, but against the official establishment and promotion of religion. The people eventually became fed up and reacted with violence.

This whole area of church-state controversy is one we have been able to avoid in the United States. We have refused to get into it by assiduously declining to use the state's coercive power for the sponsorship of support of religion. It was all but impossible for the people to become angry with the churches since the churches were in a sense merely the extension of themselves. The only churches in existence were those the people had voluntarily decided to have. For the people to be angry with the churches, therefore, was to be angry with themselves, since they had organized, financed, built and managed them. Thus, the voluntary principle in its negative aspect avoids all manner of troubles which have traditionally beset the nations. The collection plate receiving its free will gifts for the church has become the symbol of religious voluntaryism and church-state separation. Anti-clericalism can hardly exist in a country where church and state are legally separated.

It was inconceivable, however, that the traditional prerogatives of religious establishment should quickly give way to voluntaryism and church-state separation. This did not happen without a severe struggle—a struggle which still persists. Functional and financial separation of church and state, while demonstrably successful, has been exceedingly difficult to maintain. A principal cause of this difficulty has been ecclesiastical intransigence. An ecclesiastical organization that has enjoyed public subsidies and sponsorship for centuries cannot be expected to resign itself readily to their loss. It is interesting that the religious bodies which have a long tradition of establishment and tax support in other lands are the very ones which battle for the same prerogatives here.

The Roman Catholic Church is a prime example. This church has been unaccustomed to a free situation where it must compete with other religious groups. It has been used to state sponsorship with its clergy and

38

institutions financed from taxes. Leaders of this church, definitely old-world in their thinking, waged a fierce political struggle in the 1840's to get public financing for their schools. When they were resoundingly defeated they subsided for a century, then came on strong again in the 1940's. They have steadily raised the tempo of their struggle during the succeeding four decades and actually won de facto control of at least four state legislatures: Ohio, New York, Rhode Island, and Pennsylvania. They were able to force unconstitutional legislation to passage by these legislative bodies.

Behind the Roman Catholic Church in numbers and influence but not in devotion to the religious subsidy, is a militant segment of the Christian Reformed Church, possessing some political clout, particularly in the state of Michigan. The Reformed group came originally from Holland where Protestants and Catholics long ago won their battle for state subsidy and have been able to divide the schools, the politics, the business, and the culture of their country on the basis of religion. These groups together with some congregations of the Lutheran Church Missouri Synod have made a common effort to seek government financing for their denominational schools.

Together with a minor contingent of Orthodox Jews, these groups have sought to upset the American tradition of separation of church and state and along with it the principle of voluntaryism in religion.

It has proved highly fortunate that the government of the United States has a system of checks and balances. We see this advantage particularly in the three branches of government—the legislative, the executive and the judiciary. The first two are immediately responsive to pressure by voting blocs. They can readily yeild to such pressure to enact laws which they themselves know to be unconstitutional. They do this in the confidence that the Supreme Court will get them off the hook by pronouncing such laws in violation of the Constitution and therefore null and void.

Conspicuous instances of this occurred on June 28, 1971 and June 25, 1973.[1] In the former instance two lawsuits challenging state laws which provided state support for religious schools came to the Supreme Court for adjudication. If the state were to grant tax money to provide prayer books and communion equipment for churches and pay salaries of the clergy, most would agree that this was an act respecting establishment of religion. But the Court found that public funding for schools which existed for the purpose of religious indoctrination was an equally essential form of aid to religion.

To be sure, the various state plans were cunningly devised as aids to the secular educational program of the religious school. But the Supreme Court quickly penetrated this ruse and found that the aid programs lay squarely within the prohibited area.

There was definite entanglement between church and state in the aid programs of Pennsylvania and Rhode Island—entanglement such as the founders had sought to preclude by the First Amendment. The justices in their unanimous opinion made clear just what it was that was entangled. Parochial schools, they held, constitute "an integral part of the religious mission of the Catholic Church" and "they are a powerful vehicle for transmitting the Catholic faith to the next generation." And the end achieved by the laws in question was "excessive entanglement" between church and state. The Court found that ". . . the very restrictions and surveillance necessary to insure that teachers play a strictly non-ideological role give rise to entanglements between church and state." The Court made it abundantly clear that a government grant to support secular instruction in religious schools was well past the brink of the constitutionally permissible.

On June 25, 1973, the Supreme Court struck down another set of state laws carefully contrived to avoid the First Amendment ban on government aid to religion.[2] The parochiaid programs passed into law in New York, Pennsylvania and Ohio provided the following forms of parochiaid: (1) state grants to parents to reimbursement for amounts paid for tuition in a parochial school; (2) credits on income tax for tuition paid to a parochial school; (3) "mandated services"—payment to parochial schools for counting their students and performing other secretarial services for the state; (4) repair and upkeep of parochial school buildings. All were struck by a Supreme Court which had no doubt that indirect subsidies to religious schools, no less than direct subsidies, constituted aid to religion enjoined by the First Amendment.

The Court has now repeatedly held that government subsidy to religious schools, by whatever routes it may be sought, is unconstitutional. While further attempts to circumvent the establishment clause will no doubt be attempted, there would appear to be little chance of their success. At present there would seem to be no constitutional way for religious schools to draw tax support. The only way this could be brought about would be by a constitutional amendment. In view of the public sentiment which strongly supports separation of church and state, such an amendment is not a likely prospect.

There is yet another church-state problem that should be mentioned at this point, since it has resulted in a serious challenge to church-state separation. It rises, as many such threats have risen, in the area of education. The problem is personified by many religiously-dedicated persons—both Protestant and Catholic—who want to use the public schools to impose religion on the populace. The motive of these people is good. They contemplate a national moral crisis which they feel can only be met with religion. But how can the population be reached religiously? The home is failing its responsibility. The church is not reaching those who need its message.

Here, then, are the schools. Here are laws requiring all children to attend. Instead of piddling around with the limited opportunities of home and church, why not boldly seize the complete opportunity offered by the schools? Here, not some children, not a few children, are assembled, but all! What an incomparable opportunity to line up the children and

42

impose on them the religious training they need! If the complete job cannot be done, something can be done. Let the children—all of them—be given at least a whiff of religion. It could certainly do them no harm and might do worlds of good.

The error here is not hard to detect. It is, again, the tempting use of coercion in an area which must from its very nature be free. What an intriguing thought this has always been—to line up all the students under compulsory attendance laws and give them a shot of religion, just like a vaccination—to make them law abiding.

Through the 1960's and 1970's there were well coordinated and determined efforts to amend the constitutional protections of religious liberty and church-state separation with proposals which would, in effect, provide for state-mandated religion. A typical proposal for a constitutional amendment read:

"Nothing contained in this Constitution shall abridge the right of persons lawfully assembled in any public building which is supported in whole or in part through the expenditure of public funds, to participate in non-denominational prayer."

This purports to be an enabling act only: it would enable non-denominational prayer to be offered in the schools. But a quick analysis discloses the state's coercive hand. What is "non-denominational prayer"? The writer asked many religious and political leaders what "non-denominational prayer" was and he received a different answer from each. The plain fact is that nobody knew what "non-denominational prayer" was, including the sponsors of the amendment themselves. The term, "non-denominational prayer," was so bad it had to be changed during the floor debate to "voluntary prayer." This stratagem failed because it only went deeper into the mire. What is "voluntary prayer"?

This contrived obscurity meant that government would have to define the prayers that could legally be offered in public schools and require everyone to repeat them. Perhaps the government would hire teams of theological experts who would handle these religious responsibilities for the schools.

It should be noted at once that no enablement of prayer is needed. There is no ban on prayer anywhere, anytime in this country. What is banned is forced prayer—prayer imposed on people regardless of their desire. This is not only something which pertains to establishment of religion; it actually interferes with the free exercise of religion.

Enablement, in such matters, too readily becomes imposition. The government insinuates itself into religious concerns and imposes religious observances on the people. It is the state that would define and mandate the prayers to be offered in the schools. This makes a public concern of something that ought to be intimate, private and personal.

There can be no doubt what advocates of a prayer amendment want: they want mandated prayers required by government officials of all children in the schools. This was precisely the area which the architects of the First Amendment sought to close off from civil functionaries. The religion clause does not merely forbid establishment of religion. It forbids any act "respecting" this. Government is to keep its hands off the churches and its nose out of religion.

All this for a very good reason: the religious and the civil do not mix felicitously. Government must rest in the final analysis on coercion—upon its power to require men to do what appears necessary for the common good. Religion operates in quite another area—that of volition. Here men do only what they want and choose and nothing at all if that is their desire. Religion, from its very nature, must rely on voluntary choice, on the free response freely given. To be authentic, man's choices in this realm must be completely free. It follows that the area of effective religious response is the home, the church, and the personal conscience.

The advocates of the prayer amendment grimly fought to upset the nation's church-state tradition. After the prayer amendment had been defeated they tried another approach. This time they sought not passage of a constitutional amendment which would require a two-thirds majority of both houses, but a mere statute which would only need a bare majority. The proposal would limit the jurisdiction of the United States Supreme Court and the District Courts to enter any judgment, decree or order denying or restricting, as unconstitutional, voluntary prayer in any public school.

The prayer amendment was opposed by most religious groups. This is what might have been anticipated. It would be natural for the churches to defend an arrangement to which they have now grown accustomed and under which they have signally flourished. The responsible leadership of the major Protestant and Jewish groups has strongly opposed the amendment. These groups include the American and Southern Baptist Conventions, the United Methodist Church, Lutheran Church in America, United Church of Christ, Unitarian-Universalist Association, United Presbyterian Church in the U.S.A., the Episcopal Church, Presbyterian Church in the U.S., National Baptist Convention, U.S.A., National Council of Churches, Progressive Baptist Convention, American Jewish Congress, American Jewish Committee, Central Conference of American Rabbis.

There was one notable exception to this phalanx of opposition—the hierarchy of the Roman Catholic Church. This was a strange story. When the issue originally surfaced and headed for a showdown in Congress the Catholic hierarchy took a position, along with its Protestant and Jewish counterparts, critical of any prayer amendment. The National Catholic Welfare Conference (now the United States Catholic Conference) stated that the Catholic Church "continues to believe that the present clauses in the Constitution are of incalculable benefit to religion . . . . In combination, the free exercise and no establishment clauses are guarantees too vital to be tampered with lightly." (Statement issued June 16, 1964.)

This was the Catholic position held firmly during the 1971 battle in Congress. But when the issue came to the fore again in 1973, the Catholic hierarchy abruptly reversed its stand. The bishops now came forward with a statement favoring the prayer amendment. Indeed, they presented a version of their own that went far beyond anything that had been offered up to that point. Their statement issued September 20, 1973 would enable prayers in all public buildings including schools and also "religious instruction in public schools, if such instruction is provided under private auspices whether or not religious."

The cause of this sweeping change can be surmised. Between the two statements had intervened a series of decisions by the Supreme Court which had a vital bearing on church-state relations in the United States. These decisions shut off virtually all the known ways of evading the strictures of the First Amendment in regard to state support of church schools. The proposed amendment authorizing prayer and religious instruction in the public schools under private auspices offered a new approach to the Catholic drive for public subsidy to its own denominational schools. If public funds could be made available to support religious worship and instruction in public schools, then why not public funds for the same purpose in church schools? The Catholic proposal was contrived to win over to the cause of public subsidy for Catholic schools all the considerable body of public opinion that supported the prayer amendment drive.

Catholic leaders had always been apprehensive

about public school religion. Indeed, in the early 20th century Catholic plaintiffs repeatedly attacked public school religious observances as a violation of their religious freedom and as acts respecting establishment of religion.

Now that stance has been totally reversed. A powerful and respected part of the political life of the nation, the Roman Catholic leadership, now seeks to use for its own purposes the very exercise of civil authority it once sought to escape. It sees now a chance to use this authority to its own advantage—to impose its own religious practices in public institutions and to finance such practices in its own institutions. The aim here signals a reversion to the coercive mentality of the Roman Catholic Church which has historically welcomed the arm of the state as an aid in imposing religious faith (its own version) upon the populace.

The pathetic thing about such use of the state's coercion is that it undermines the church's power of attraction. It erodes the church's ability to win voluntary response from the people. In its absorption with the instant method of coercion, the church forgets the tremendous opportunities in the area of volition. The drive for a government prayer amendment provides a clear instance. It is the ease of the thing that impresses. No tortuous appeals. No grueling evangelism. No house to house canvass, no person to person contacts. Reach every one in a hurry by passing a law. Save time and trouble; just regiment everybody. Line them up and give them all a shot of religion. Provide a quick cure for society's ills.

What we see here is a classic example of something worse than bigotry. Here are those who "know what is best" for everybody. They will use public authority and public agencies to force their religious views on the populace. What can we say of this effort? There is something almost sadistic about it. It is basically an effort of certain people to compel others to watch them pray. Not only must they watch, pressure is exerted to make them join in. Forced prayer defeats the whole purpose of prayer—which, by its very nature, is private, and above all, voluntary. Prayer is definitely not an exercise to be imposed upon the reluctant. Effective prayer can only take its rise from a voluntary act. The greatest authority on prayer tells us to practice it privately. "Go into your room," he said, "shut the door, and pray to your Father who is in secret . . . . "[3]

Rather than lamenting the closure of public programs of prayer, religionists should rejoice in the tremendous opportunities that are available. These opportunities should be used. The writer believes in prayer. He not only believes in it, he practices it. In his home prayer has been practiced every day for many years. Note this significant fact: the government has never once interfered with these prayers! The home is the natural place for prayer as millions have discerned. Government is halted by its own constitutional inhibitions from interfering. All across the land churches have been built and people regularly gather in them for prayer. Government has never interfered with any of this. It is all freely done.

During the incumbency of the late President John

F. Kennedy there was a decision of the Supreme Court barring compulsory prayer in the schools of New York State.[4] What was barred was not prayer itself but a prayer demanded by the state of all public school children. The requirement was judged by the Court to be an act respecting establishment of religion and was struck. A wave of savage vituperation swept the land. The very idea that children could not be compelled to pray in public schools! It was an outrage! President Kennedy said just nine words which calmed the nation. He said: "We can still pray at home and in church." Just so, but is seems so easy to forget.

Here we encounter the real peril of proposals like the prayer amendment. Such an enactment would push government into a hornet's nest. It would embroil thousands of communities in religious strife. It would spark religious controversies which even the wisdom of Solomon could not resolve. Consider the Regent's Prayer in New York State mentioned above. The prayer reads as follows: "Almighty God, we acknowledge our dependence upon Thee, and we ask Thy blessing upon us, our children, our parents, our teachers and our country."

That was prescribed utterance for all school children in New York State. That was it, nothing more. Who could take offense? Who would burn with shame and outrage at the prospect of having to repeat this innocuous utterance at the beginning of the school day? The schools' directors foresaw no problems. No one would pay any attention. No one would care. How totally wrong they were! This mauve utterance stirred fierce animosities in one community after another, set brother against brother, and brought antagonists into a court battle that raged all the way to the Supreme Court of the United States.

Abington v. Schempp was a lawsuit which resulted from a Pennsylvania program of reading a few verses from the Bible together with a brief prayer at the start of each school day.[5] Here, again, community resentments were aroused and a struggle persisted—all the way to the nation's highest Court.

There is a lesson here: religion is an area where government ought to keep out. If this seemingly harmless prayer and modest Bible reading could produce such pandemonium, one can only surmise what monumental bitterness would accrue from more comprehensive efforts of a similar nature. When will mankind learn that religion is an area where coercion is never appropriate? It seems so obvious. What have the centuries taught if they have not taught this fact? In the area of religion, men can be kindled, inspired, led—but never coerced. Yet the religious coercionists are with us still. They seek to force others into their own mold, and, like the road to hell, their path is paved with the very best intentions.

Proponents of compulsory prayer plead the "free exercise" argument. But free exercise cannot be carried to the point of compulsory worship. To compel students to attend school and worship there is no different, in principle, from compelling them to go to church and worship there. The one is as wrong as the other. It is not alone a matter of the Constitution; it is a

51

question of what is right and it is a question of what will work. Again we encounter the futility of coercion in religion. For religion to be an effective force in a person's life it must be voluntarily embraced and pursued.

We see another serious invasion of the realm of personal choice in a proposed constitutional amendment which would approve laws to be passed prohibiting a woman from having an abortion. The drive commenced after a decision of the Supreme Court on January 22, 1973 which struck down certain state laws limiting abortion rights. The Supreme Court steered a careful course refusing to endorse "abortion on demand," but recognizing the woman's basic right to determine whether or not she should have a child. This right obtained through the first three months of pregnancy. In the period between the third and seventh months, states may regulate the medical factors of abortion but may not make it unavailable. During the final ten weeks of pregnancy states may regulate or even forbid abortions save for those necessary to preserve the life of the mother.

The decision was not only theoretically but practically sound. There is hardly any prerogative that identifies more intimately with a woman's decision making than the matter of child bearing. The suggestion that the state has authority to step in and dictate on such a matter seems bizarre on the face. The fact that the nation's largest church officially advocates this point of view completes the irony.

Government cannot run everything and should

not try to do so. When government seeks to preempt the decision-making in regard to conception and birth, this is too much. Of course government cannot really do this, but it can try as it has so often done in the past. Government has sought to police this area of human conduct, often banning abortions altogether. This prohibition has not halted abortions. It has merely made them illegal and decreed that they be carried out under dangerous and barbarous conditions.

There are those who argue from labored theological presuppositions that a fetus at conception is a human personality with all the rights pertaining thereto. This is simply not so and common sense repudiates it. Common sense tells us that a human personality is not a human personality until it becomes one at birth. It is an incredible error to confuse a uterine blob with a human personality possessed of all personal rights and privileges.

When governmental coercion seeks to intervene in this area with its regulation, this is all wrong. It is a classic example of its being where it has no business to be. Such a matter as whether or not to have an abortion should rest squarely with the woman involved. It inheres by natural right in her own decision making. It is a matter of religious and civil liberty. For government to insinuate itself into her affairs at this point, telling her what she may or may not do, is an intrusion that cannot be tolerated.

The 1973 decision of the Supreme Court striking down various bans and limitations on abortion was one of the best common sense pronouncements ever to come from that body. The decision was eminently fair and reasonable. It did not require or encourage any woman to have an abortion. What is did was to permit her, in consultation with her physician and within reasonable time limits, to have an abortion if she so desired. That is exactly as it should be. For this is a private area which conspicuously calls for the personal decision.

It is the voluntary principle that stands at the heart of religious faith. The moment voluntaryism gives way to compulsion the edge is gone. Religion is more characteristically caught than taught. If it is effective at all, it has a power of attraction which draws adherents with a kind of magnetism. They embrace it because they find in it that which feeds their own spiritual needs. There is no need here to compel. It is like a man coming to a feast. To impose religion by force or coercion is to lose it altogether. If religion cannot win its way in a free climate, no amount of official compulsion can be of any possible benefit.

Northern Ireland today provides a classic example of the impotence of compulsory religion. Worship and religious instruction are required performances in both public (Protestant) and Catholic schools. Despite this, the two groups go on slaughtering each other and demonstrate a total incapacity to work out some kind of *modus vivendi*. Someone has remarked that he wished all Irishmen were atheists so that they could live together like Christians! Perhaps that is unfair, but it is not unfair to point to Northern Ireland as a classic failure of compulsory religion in the schools.

Billy Graham sees the inception of a fourth "Great Awakening" in "para-church movements" of recent years—prayer meetings, Bible study groups, religious groups among students and professional athletes.

A plethora of Christian, quasi-Christian and other religious groups have sprung into existence in recent years. Some of these are Scientology, Edgar Cayce's Association for Research and Enlightenment, Transcendental Meditation, Servants of the Light, Hare Krishna, Worldwide Church of God, Children of God, Zen Buddhism, Meher Baba, Bahai G-O, Rosicrucians, Unity, Unification Church, Soka Gokkai, Church of the Final Judgment, Yuga, Subud and scores of others. Perhaps one might cite a less benign direction of cultism represented by such as Spiritualism, Witchcraft and Satanism.

All of these are strictly voluntary movements thriving in a country which permits free exercise of religion. It can be argued that some of these movements are evil and produce harmful effects. Yet the overall effects of "free exercise" are good. People are inspired to dedicate themselves to significant personal goals and discipline themselves in their pursuit. For the most part this is to the good.

Another major challenge to voluntary religion has been posed by the ecumenical movement of the 1960's and 1970's. This movement offered the uninspired spectacle of denominational leaders vieing with one another in surrendering their distinctives in order to join a gray consensus. The strength of the religious enterprise has traditionally been exhibited not in pale homogeneity but in vital proliferation. Religious leaders who readily yield their group's distinctives in favor of some supposed ecumenical value do not serve the cause of religion. What religion needs today is less homogenity and more variety, not one big, dull church, but a lot of vital little ones. Mergers always result in the impoverishment of the participants. They lose their own distinctives in the process and these are their source of their strength.

What the religious scene in America needs is "not peace but a sword"—not ecumenism and merger but more division! Perhaps not division so much as new departures. Fortunately, such a development is taking place. Even as the ecumenical movement saps the vitality of the churches, a proliferation of vital sects has developed in great force. It is characterized first by a rapid growth of certain smaller churches and the appearance of a variety of new ones which flourish even as the larger communions languish. As viewed at this moment, the future is not with the merger-mad ecumenists who will surrender anything for togetherness, but with the devout conservatives who believe something and will stand up for it.

The stultifying effect of ecumenism is demonstrated by the National Council of Churches which has become increasingly inclusive in its membership, taking in the Orthodox and eventually reaching out to the Roman Catholic Church as well. While the latter was reluctant to go all the way to full membership and participation in the Council, it did enter into a working union with Council leaders. How the Catholic leaders expected to use this relationship was quickly demonstrated.

The National Council had a long record of opposition to federal aid to parochial schools. When a proposal of a tax credit plan to achieve this purpose surfaced in Congress in 1973 the National Council naturally came out against it. They had always opposed this sort of thing and they were merely recording their traditional position. But the Catholic leadership was furious, assumed a hurt stance, denounced the National Council and declared that all liaisons with it would be ended forthwith. The Catholic Conference executive secretary, Bishop James Rausch, made it plain that he had expected all Council statements to be cleared with him before they were issued. He obviously conceived of ecumenism as a method of bringing other groups over to his denomination's point of view. To cap the climax, National Council's executive secretary apologized abjectly, stopping just short of disowning the Council's position. It is not a coincidence that the National Council and its member churches, too, are definitely in recession. A church organization that will not stand up for its convictions cannot hope to thrive.

We see the problem at the local level in Hartford, Connecticut where there was a proposal to enlarge the Council of Churches to take in the Catholic parishes to this traditionally Protestant association. The Catholic Archbishop John T. Whealen refused the invitation initially because the Council had gone on record as opposed to government subsidy to parochial schools. Such a statement was in conflict with Catholic views and the Catholic Church could not be associated with any organization which espoused it. "No problem," said Council officials. They would rescind the statement and agree not to issue any statement in the future that would displease the diocese. The Rev. David E. Chambers, president of the Council, explained: "We are trying to reach out to include all bodies."

The formula for inclusion was clear: give up everything anybody objected to. The ecumenical ideal is equally apparent: include everybody and give up everything.

Sure enough: the Greater Hartford Council of Churches endorsed transformation to a pallid relic by a resounding vote 108 to 46. Henceforth the Council will amount to exactly nothing and everybody knows it. It has its built-in guarantee of sterile nonentity. Someone has suggested as a slogan for the new, enlarged Council: "Better nothing than something."

We see the ecumenical thing in its stark naivete in a statement of Irish Bishop H. R. McAdoo:

> "You can walk into a small Irish village and see three churches—Roman Catholic, Anglican and Methodist—when there are hardly enough people to fill one church. What a wonderful thing it would be if they were all part of one thing together."[6]

Why so? What is so wonderful about eliminating some small churches to make bigger ones? If this is done—as it always has been done—by the surrender of distinctives in favor of bland consensus, where is the gain? The logical end is to do away with the entire religious operation—simply bland it out into nothing.

Another point of difference is in the matter of birth control. Most Protestant denominations have taught the desirability of birth control in family planning and have often cooperated in establishing and maintaining clinics where birth control advice and equipment are provided. The Catholic Church has continued its official ban on what it calls "artificial" birth control and has reiterated the position since the Vatican Council. The Encyclical of Pope Paul VI *Humanae Vitae* issued following Vatican Council II on July 25, 1968 makes it clear that all effective birth control procedures are barred to the faithful. If ecumenism were to score a victory and the Catholic and Protestant agencies were to form a working alliance, the birth control clinics would have to be terminated as objectionable to the Catholic leaders. The fact that in practice most Catholics sensibly reject their church's anti-birth control teaching would not really help the situation. The clinics would likely be a casualty. It would be another case of paralysis via ecumenism.

The insistence of the Catholic bishops on a legal ban on all abortions offers another case in point. Other groups joining the ecumenical movement under the Catholic aegis would be expected to surrender this basic religious and civil liberty—the right to have an abortion—if this seemed necessary and desirable.

It is not in ecumenism but in proliferation that the church becomes vital. A classic example is provided by the Protestant Reformation. The Reformation hit the church with shattering force, creating divisions which still exist. Far from being a disaster, this was a fortuitous event. For the Reformation had the salubrious effect of shattering beyond repair the strangling tyranny of the Pope over the church and the classic union of this power with that of the state in various countries. This enabled developments of many kinds to take place. Sad to relate, the Lutheran and Reformed movements rather quickly joined themselves to various political rulers and lost their creative drive. Yet the sectarian development continued to vitalize the church with its power even as it had in the past. Arians, Albigensians, Waldensians, Lollards, Hussites, Calvinists, Anabaptists, Quakers, Methodists, Campbellites represent the creative edge of the church. They represent dissidence rather than conformity, but without them the church would have been a dry and dismal thing. Proliferation was proof of vitality. For if people believe in something to the point of dissent this is evidence that they really believe it. And, when people really believe, their belief is vital.

The vitality of the religious enterprise is demonstrated by a resurgence of sectarian power. Unsophisticated fundamentalist sects like the Seventh-day Adventists, the Assemblies of God, the Church of the Nazarene, the Church of God, the Evangelical Free Church and all the Pentecostal groups show impressive gains in all categories. The large Southern Baptist Convention has retained much of its primitive strength. Yet, even here there are foreboding signs. Its rate of growth has slowed and a sector of its leadership has evidenced an eagerness for public subsidy. Ecumenism is also touching the Southern Baptists with its enervating hand. The Church of Jesus Christ of Latter Day Saints (Mormon) is the one other major group that continues to register substantial gains. It is strictly non-ecumenical.

New groups like the Jesus Movement suddenly appear. It is a spontaneous thing, apparently without connecting links or a national base. The movement erupts in many communities with strong appeal for the young. It is not uncommon to observe neighborhood Bible study groups without any tie to a particular denomination. Personnel of the armed services are also meeting in such informal groups for Bible study and mutual encouragement in the Christian life. Even as the established churches fade, there are fresh outbursts of religious concern. "Drive-in" churches thrive in informal settings. Communes appear in all major cities. "Jesus freaks" roam the streets zealously seeking dialogue with all who will confront them and making converts along the way. "Born again" Christians turn up everywhere. Record crowds of teenagers throng public coliseums for large religious services. Thousands, once caught up in a hippie culture of drugs and crime, find hope.

It is, to be sure, inevitable that religion should be organized. This is an entirely logical development. It is equally true that the organizing process which regularizes religion also tends to paralyze it and may mark its demise. Yet the redemptive possibilities of the Christian faith have proved most formidable.

Something in it perenially breaks loose from its atrophied forms and bursts out into new expressions. Voluntary enterprise has saved religion from apparently sure doom time and time again. The saving ventures have themselves become sterile only to be shocked to new life by an unpredictable resurgence.

The devotion of the American people to religion is demonstrated by the magnitude of their donations. According to the American Association of Fund-Raising Counsel, Americans contributed $12.84 billion to their churches in 1976.

While religion presents by all odds the most impressive and most productive of voluntary enterprises, there are many others. Free Masonry is a classic example. Transplanted from Europe in Colonial times, these virile groups maintained by the devotion of their members played a significant role in the emergence of the United States as an independent nation and world power. Fortunately, they never became attached to the poltical authority.

Indeed, the voluntary principle which includes religion has a much broader incidence in the United States. Alex de Tocqueville, famous French observer of the United States in the nineteenth century, was struck by the American penchant for voluntary associations. He noted that, whereas in other countries government would undertake most necessary responsibilities, in America it would often be done by a voluntary group.[7] Nothing is more distinctly American than our voluntaryism in social endeavors. This has repeatedly made possible innovations which the public sector inhibited by its very width could not have initiated. A prime example is birth control, which by the broad spectrum of public opinion was originally closed to public programs. Thanks to private organizations, such programs could operate, gain favor, and eventually be approved for public operation.

It is estimated that there are as many as 6 million private, voluntary organizations in the United States.[8] The list includes 350,000 religious organizations. Many of these are "do good" groups established for special philanthropic purposes.

The National Center for Voluntary Action estimates that some $26 billion in volunteer time is donated annually through voluntary agencies.[9]

Government itself sometimes recognizes the advantages of voluntaryism. Wilbur J. Cohen, a former Secretary of Health, Education and Welfare, has called attention to the continuing need for voluntary effort to innovate "in areas where public agencies lack knowledge or are afraid to venture . . . . The private sector is adept at innovation and at providing the models government needs."[10]

Michael Novak, the columnist, has marveled at the volume of voluntary goodness that surfaces in this country: "The amount of sheer giving, voluntary activity, and non-profit creative energy under our system is one of the great marvels of international life."[11]

The role of the service clubs—Rotary, Lions, Kiwanis, Ruritan, and others—is well known. Also a plethora of societies and corporations organized to promote many worthy causes. Such additional organizations as the YMCA and YWCA, Boy Scouts and Girl Scouts, Goodwill Industries, various veterans' groups, hospital auxiliaries, PTA's and an infinite number of auxiliaries, guilds, etc. bring people together for a variety of good works. These groups are many and highly diverse, but they belong, with the churches, to a precious segment of our culture, a segment sparked by voluntaryism. Not only would society be poorer without them, it probably could not exist as we know it without them. All are strictly voluntary groups which exist only by virtue of individuals' desire to come together to do good.

While such "do good" associations are not altogether free of self-interest, they are basically so. Such groups have no official status or connection. They have nothing to do with government. The state's compulsion is not involved in their programs in any way.

In a civilization such as ours there can be no substitute for the redemptive operation of the voluntary principle. A people whose gaze is fixed on Washington and government programs would do well to seek a new focus. they would do better to join a group of like-minded "causers" and help make something happen. Such are the free, voluntary associations. They constitute a vital element of the nation's strength.

1. *Lemon v. Kurtzman,* 403 U.S. 602 (1971).
   Earley v. Di Censo, 403 U.S. 602 (1971).
   Pearl v. Nyquist, 72-269, 72-270, 72-271, Sup. Ct. (1973)
   Lemon v. Sloan, 93 Sup. Ct. 2982 (1973).
2. *Pearl v. Nyquist, op. cit.*
   Lemon v. Sloan, op. cit.
   Kosydar v. Wolman, Civil Action Nos. 72-212 and 72-222, Affirmed by Sup. Ct.
3. Matthew 6:5.
4. *Engel v. Vitale,* 370 U.S. 426 (1962).
5. *Abington v. Schempp,* 374 U.S. 203 (1963).
6. *Religious News Service,* April 5, 1974.
7. Alex de Tocqueville, *Democracy in America,* Vol. 2, 1906, p. 106.
8. *Giving in America: Report of the Commission on Private Philantrophy and Public Needs,* 1975, p. 36.
9. *Guide to Sponsored Research of the Commission on Private Philanthropy and Public Needs,* 1975, p. 15.
10. *Ibid.,* p. 42
11. *Washington Star,* December 21, 1976.

4. Free Exercise of Religion

Often separation of church and state is celebrated negatively: how wonderful it is that nobody has to have any particular religion—or any religion at all! One can be an atheist and government will do nothing whatever about it. But what about the other side of the coin? One can be enthusiastically religious according to any of the existing versions, or he can come up with a new one. He has complete freedom in these matters. Government has pledged itself not to interfere or impede and, indeed, to permit religion's free exercise in every possible way.

In according free exercise to religion the United States government has bestowed its greatest boon. "Congress shall make no law prohibiting the free exercise (of religion)." Free exercise—freedom to do anything which does not trespass on the rights of others. And freedom from government sponsorship and patronage—that arch-foe of religion! For there is no speedier way to chill religion than to mingle it with the coercion of government. This combination promptly drains religion of its spontaneity and its prophetic unction. Official requirement kills the joy of voluntary response. This is the truth to which the Supreme Court of Ohio pointed in a decision handed down in 1872:

" . . . United with government, religion never rises above the merest superstition; united with religion, government never rises above the merest despotism; and all history shows us that the more widely and completely they are separated, the better it is for both."[1]

The redemptive, creative power of religion appears almost beyond belief. A religious leader can work wonders, whether he be crank, crook, or authentic prophet. As a result of the power he unleashes the corrupt can become virtuous, the shiftless dedicated and the rootless firmly anchored. Indeed, such results can ensue even though the leader himself may turn out to be an ego-maniac of the worst sort. Despite unworthy personal traits, he may possess a gift for exploding and setting off the redemptive force of religion. Such leaders are channels through which this power flows.

There has to be organization, of course—some means for conserving and systematizing what has been wrought. The charismatic leader is sometimes good at organization, too. St. Paul and John Wesley are examples. This would appear to be the perfect combination. The trouble is that the leader's successors, invariably lacking his charisma, depend on system and order. This is not enough. Or, they may seek to utilize the legalism of the state to impose their discipline, raise their funds and otherwise insure their survival. This is worse, for it quickly drains the movement of its vitality and insures its prompt demise as a regenerative force though it may nominally survive for centuries.

It is volition that kindles religion, coercion that strangles it. There is nothing more delightful to the human spirit than doing what it really wants and longs to do. In every human being there are vistas of moral and spiritual achievement rarely touched. They are there waiting for a redemptive power to set them off. Souls listen eagerly for a voice inviting them to take up their cross and follow. Their capacity for shaping up and accepting such an invitation staggers belief. Once buried in sin, they walk in righteousness; once blind, they see; once dead, they awaken to newness of life.

Here we leave behind the sepulchral rule of law and enter the realm of grace. The law is necessary, a sine qua non of human existence. It enables mankind to survive after a fashion. Without it chaos and death would be inevitable. But it is only by grace—the glory of a voluntary response to the divine invitation—that human beings really come alive. When this happens we see religion in its true light functioning as the Creator intended. Free exercise is the lifeblood of religion.

What are some of the tangible expressions of government's concern for the free exercise of religion in the United States? Tax exemption for houses of worship is a ready example. Every state in the Union provides such an exemption—even though churches utilize the services that taxes on other property support. Such services as police and fire protection, water and sewer service, and also education, are commonly sustained by the real estate tax. Exemption for churches, and often parsonages and rectories as well, enables churches to omit a considerable item from their budget each year.

Indeed, so helpful has the tax exemption proved for the churches that the exemption has been challenged in the courts as constituting an act respecting establishment of religion and also as violating the "equal protection" of non-religious taxpayers. This was the contention in the *Walz* case.[2] Here the charge was that in encouraging free exercise the government had actually gone into the business of promoting and establishing religion. The Court did not see it that way; it upheld the religious exemption as a part of a large class of charitable, educational and eleemosynary institutions serving the public welfare.

Tax policy in the United States goes even further. Donations to churches are included along with donations to many other charitable causes as exempt items in the calculation of one's income tax up to 50 per cent of taxable income. Thus, one may enjoy some reduction in what he is required to pay the government in terms of amounts he has paid for the support of religion.

This encouragement to free exercise is seen in

classic form in the military chaplaincy. In the United States the chaplaincy has always been considered as the inveterate companion of military conscription. As men were drafted into the service they were, of course, removed from their homes and communities. In many respects this was an irretrievable separation and nothing could be done about it. There was a sharp break with the community and home for which the military could not compensate.

In regard to religion, however, something could be done. The military chaplaincy was the answer. It is by no means a perfect answer. It may not even be a very good answer. One can quickly criticize it on a dozen counts. But it is something. It is an effort to fill a gaping void in men's life when they are abruptly taken from their communities and, in effect, denied the free exercise of religion. A religious opportunity is created for them and made available. They need not avail themselves of it. Most of them do not. But it is there if and when they want it.

Prison chaplaincies serve free exercise even more obviously. When men have to be put away and locked up in order to protect society, their religious opportunities are seriously inhibited at the very time they need them most. The prison chaplaincy is an effort to compensate at this point. Again, the effort is admittedly inadequate, but it is something. It is with all its frailities a compensatory form of free exercise of religion made available by the state.

The chaplaincies in the United States Senate and House of Representatives cannot be justified in the

71

same way. They are not agencies of free exercise and possibly border on official establishment of religion. But they have one powerful argument going for them—tradition. We have always had these chaplaincies. Certainly they were there before the First Amendment was ever drafted. They were the product of an era when the services of religion were much less available than they are today. The chaplaincy persists because it is easier to have it than to go through the business of doing away with it. Who wants to leap to his feet in Congress with a motion to eliminate the chaplaincy? There are far more productive horses to ride. Hence Congressional chaplaincy continues as an extension of free exercise which approaches the perimeters of establishment.

We have already mentioned the encouragement for religious donations provided in tax law. The Internal Revenue Code contains other encouragements to the free exercise of religion. Note, for example, its treatment of the clergy who are given many tax breaks. The clergyman's housing and his food, under certain circumstances, are tax exempt. If a clergyman belongs to an order which includes among its commitments a vow of poverty, his salary from any source whatever goes, without withholding tax, to his church.

Another break for the churches in the Code is the provision which enables a donor to give highly appreciated stocks or other assets to a church and be credited with tax deductions at full market value without any capital gains tax. This is a break for such individual taxpayers, but it also provides enormous encouragement for donations to churches and other charities.

One of the most sensational breaks which the Code bestows on churches is immunity in the ordinary run from the requirement of public financial reports. Unless something goes wrong and there is a special problem, churches are not required to provide such reports at all and many of them do not. If there is a scandal or some challenge is raised, the Internal Revenue Service can authorize an investigation. But this can be done only at the level of a regional Director and can only concern itself with the immediate problem. The churches are the only organizations which enjoy this immunity.

Here we have yet another example of how government in this country gives churches many kinds of advantages in its tax laws. Why does it do so? It seeks to provide every precaution against any inhibition of the free exercise of religion. Taxes are not to inhibit free exercise, nor are reports, disclosure, and all the various requirements to which other corporations and individuals are subjected by the Internal Revenue Service. Some of this may sound like acts respecting establishment of religion, but it is all done in the name of free exercise.

The question is raised: under our system how free is religion? And the answer might well be given: under our system religious groups are free to do anything! There are almost literally no restraints on the kind of performance that will be tolerated provided it assumes a religious stance. The only limits would be those of

73

public health and welfare. A performance that interfered with the rights of others might lead to restraint, but there is no limit on anything short of that.

On only a few occasions have those limits been breached. One thinks of the Mormon polygamous marriages and the famous Reynolds case in which their legality was challenged. Eventually, the government moved against the plural marriages of this sect which outraged the monogamous standard of the community. But the Mormons had their day before the nation's highest Court.[3] The eventual decision was that plural marriages, even though advocated by one's church, were damaging to the community. The Court ordered their termination.

When charged with distributing hallucinatory drugs to young people, Dr. Timothy Leary asserted that this was a sacrament of his religion. This defense might seem to be good for little more than a cynical laugh, yet the government took it in deadly earnest and the issue went to the Supreme Court. Where free exercise of religion may possibly be concerned, there is no fooling around. Under our system the most outrageous behavior has a chance at legality if it pleads that religion is involved. Navajo Indians claimed that their use of the hallucinatory drug peyote was sacramental and basic to the free exercise of their tribal religion. The California Supreme Court agreed and refused to permit interference with the Navajo rites. One can scarcely think of anything more destructive of human good than the drinking of cyanide and the handling of poisonous reptiles. Yet both these

74

performances have claimed immunity under the free exercise clause with appropriate Biblical quotations to support them. They have had their day in the courts, too, before the Supreme Court of Tennessee finally outlawed them on the ground that the state has "the right to guard against the unnecessary creation of widows and orphans." Our political system has undoubtedly tolerated a great deal of foolishness because it called itself by the name of religion. It has done so rather than risk any trespass upon free exercise.

We find ourselves, then, in a perpetually uneasy balance between the Scylla of free exercise and the Charybdis of no establishment. What the law may not impede or restrain, it may not promote. Where is the line of demarkation? How do we strike the balance? The word "respecting" is crucial to the religion clause. "Congress"—and this now extends via the Fourteenth Amendment to every official body in the United States—"shall make no law *respecting* an establishment of religion or forbidding the free exercise thereof." What is forbidden is not merely an establishment of religion. What is forbidden is anything which pertains to this, anything which relates to this or concerns this or points in this direction.

What is permissible, on the other hand, is not that which aids religion but that which permits religion to aid itself. A government subsidy for churches would be aid to religion. Mr. Walz' attorney argued before the Supreme Court that a tax exemption to a church was tantamount to a government subsidy since it was the same thing cashwise. The Court disagreed. The difference lay in subsequent surveillance and the entanglement which this involved. A subsidy requires the continuing ties to see that the money is used according to law. This is the case with all public expenditures and those for the churches would be no exception. A tax exemption, on the other hand, is given and that is the end of the matter. It is over and done. The churches are given an advantage, to be sure, but only one that facilitates the doing of their own work, whatever that work may be. Tax exemption is not government doing something for the churches so much as it is government enabling the churches to do something for themselves. It is an encouragement to voluntaryism.

We see the same principle involved in the other First Amendment rights guaranteed to the people. There are to be no laws abridging freedom of speech, press or assembly. This does not mean that if a man wants to make a speech the government will hire a hall or put him on a television network. A freedom to do something is quite different from a government subsidy to pay for doing it. Freedom of the press does not mean that government will pay for the printing and distribution of everybody's ideas.

What is granted here is bare freedom—the right to believe, do and proclaim what seems good and true. The freedom proffered is an inducement to the individual or the group to produce what they are capable of producing. For religious groups this means not only the right to entertain certain ideas but the right to communicate and promote them as well. Put in religious terminology, this means the right to propagate one's faith, the right to evangelize.

Free exercise for the church begins with the freedom to meet as a group for worship. It includes the right to receive donations free of income tax, the right to acquire and hold tax-free property and erect houses of worship and, as we have noted, the right to witness and make converts. All of these are contingent rights. They are contingent on the people's doing something with them. The rights exist but they exist only subject to exercise. Unless they are exercised by the people themselves out of their own desire and choice they have no reality. In practical effect there would be no religion without the free exercise which gives it substance.

There are some disadvantages and dangers in such a system. One heavy consequence of the free, open situation is that wide tolerance of religious kooks and freaks is mandatory. In a completely free situation, some silly choices will inevitably be made and some wierdo groups are likely to appear and thrive. What to do? Let them play themselves out. Let them proceed till they fall over their own feet and collapse of their own weight. It happens all the time. One religious group after another disintegrates and disappears while its contemporaries flourish. Free exercise buries the failures as surely as it crowns the successes. This leads to a far more satisfactory resolution of the matter than, for example, the "deprogramming" of young people whose parents or guardians feel they have made a wrong choice. The courts will likely disapprove of deprogramming as interference with free exercise of religion.

Understanding of the American system grows as it is compared with that of Soviet Russia. There are certain formal similarities between our arrangement in church-state affairs and that of the Soviet Union. Soviet leaders have insisted that separation of church and state was largely the same in the U.S.S.R. and the United States and point to similar constitutional provisions. Yet, in practice the difference is enormous. The Soviets have freedom of worship; the United States has that and something which goes far beyond that— the free exercise of religion. All this became very real to the writer during an interview with the Soviet Council for Religious Affairs which handles all such matters in the Soviet Union.

In the Soviet Union any group of worshippers can indicate their desire for a meeting place. If they are willing to meet certain commitments for taxes, insurance, repair and maintenance, etc. they can have it. In this place they can hold worship services—as many as they want. But that is all. No Bible classes for young people—you can be jailed for that—no making of converts, no evangelism, no missions, no radio, only rigidly controlled printed materials, no outreach. All this kind of activity is rigidly banned and people are regularly jailed for violations of the law.

What the Soviets are doing, hopefully, is to allow religion to play itself out. Those who want it can have it.

The masters of this Marxist state see religion as in a phasing out process. They hope it will die. They are confident that it will die. But they will not beat it to death. Meanwhile, if there are those who want this dying phenomenon, let them have it. It will do less harm than to extinguish the faintly glowing embers with violence. Meanwhile, it is atheistic propaganda that is given free exercise in the Soviet Union. It is the atheists who have access to press and media. It is the atheists who possess all the liberties enjoyed by religionists in the United States. In the light of Russian history one can observe that the Soviets would be more likely to provide government subsidies for the church than to permit the free exercise of religion. It is one thing to subsidize a church and in the process to apply control and direction. It is something else to turn religion loose with freedom to develop as it can and will. We need not be surprised, therefore, to note that most Communist governments, like other totalitarian dictatorships, regularly subsidize church institutions and the clergy. What better way to control them?

Protagonists of state sponsored religion love to point out that the United States is one of the few civilized countries where religion is left to its own without state aid. As they argue, religion must be considered too important a matter to be left to chance. Since the condition of religion so vitally relates to that of the state, it follows that religion must be cared for and properly nurtured and protected by the state. This attitude has almost consistently prevailed in Christendom since the official establishment of the Christian religion by the Roman Emperor Constantine in 325 A.D.

Those who see separation of church and state as a highly exceptional arrangement among the nations are correct. The mentality that officializes religion establishes it as a national norm and subsidizes its operations is generally characteristic of the western world. We see the persistence of this concept even today in countries which, though officially atheistic, continue, nevertheless, to subsidize the clergy and institutions of the church. They do so from the force of long habit. It is the sort of thing that self-respecting political regimes are supposed to do. It is a method for assuring effective control. To reject this entire concept and to make a virtue of the rejection—this is something new under the sun.

Exceptional and amazing is the no establishment-free exercise concept. Here religion sinks or swims entirely on its own. Indeed, religion has swum very well in this free situation. Houses of worship ranging from handsome temples to unadorned meeting houses are to be seen in every American community. These churches house almost every conceivable kind of worship. But all have one characteristic in common: they were wanted by people. They are there because some people donated the funds, the time, the leadership to put them there. If their interest dies, the church, too, will die and the property will be put to other uses.

We see a classic instance of this development in the use of Roman Catholic denominational schools. These institutions have been dying at a rapid rate. Some of this decline is due to the falling birthrate among the Catholic people. But more of it is due to changing priorities of Catholic parents, who, for reasons that seem good to them no longer desire separate, sectarian schools for their children. Also, there is the decline in the number of teaching nuns whose ranks have been reduced by nearly one-half in the past decade. Since these persons teach for cost-of-living salaries, the financial impact on the parochial schools is obvious.

The reaction of the Catholic clerical leadership has been to turn to government, as though government subsidies would solve the problems of their schools. Government spending on the parochial schools might have an impact initially helpful. It might keep some of these institutions functioning for a time. But the overall effect would be to aggravate the problems rather than to solve them.

Look for a moment at these problems and their possible causes. Teaching nuns of the various religious orders are leaving their posts and renouncing their vows to the church. The number of new recruits is at an all-time low. Why is this? Outsiders do not know and insiders are quite as baffled. Whatever the cause, it is obviously spiritual and religious in nature. The spiritual leverage which once impelled young people to a life of service to their church has lost its power. They do not feel something that was very real to their predecessors.

Likewise with Catholic parents. What was the force which once impelled them at great sacrifice to educate their children in separate schools of their denomination? What has happened that so many of them now prefer to have their children mingle with those of other faiths in common schools? It should be noted that the decline of Catholic schools is even more rapid in the affluent suburbs than in the indigent inner city. Obviously, this is more than a money problem. It is a spiritual problem, a religious problem. And again, a kind of problem to which government patronage has no relevance. Why should government undertake to shore up denominational schools whose own votaries no longer want them? All such problems find their origin and solution deep in the voluntary recesses of man's being. Given a modicum of effective management, such problems are resolved when spirits are kindled and persons respond. Even the cleverest management and the most lavish outlays of government subsidy will not save parochial schools if the Catholic people do not really want them.

A friend remarked recently: "What the Catholic Church needs is not government subsidy but a revival of religion!" And Protestants need it too! It is the re-kindling of religious fervor which actuates the voluntary principle. It is when people are stirred spiritually that they make commitments and keep them. It is in the throes of such experience that they become willing to dedicate themselves to their church, taking vows of poverty, chastity, and obedience. Again, spirits must be kindled by warm devotion if parents are to undergo the added cost and effort to place their children in the separate schools of their church. One really has to believe fervently. To win such commitments the church must exercise a great power of attraction for individuals. When it loses this, no official sponsorship or government promotion can take its place.

The freedom to seek such commitment from believers without the state's interference constitutes the ultimate opportunity for religion. It is made freely available to all religious groups in the United States. That is what the "free exercise" clause of the First Amendment is all about.

Footnotes

1. *Board of Education v. Minor*, Ohio Supreme Court, 23 Ohio St. 211 (1972).
2. *Walz v. New York Tax Commissioner*, 397 U.S. 664 (1970).
3. *Reynolds v. United States*, 98 U.S. 145 (1878).

5. The Task of Religion

Society flourishes when its component of voluntary leaderhip is strong and wise. It declines and even falls into ruin when this vital ingredient is lacking.

Of course, government with its compulsion is ever with us and necessarily so. As we have conceded, there could be no decent society and probably no society of any kind without compulsion. Society sets the rules. If people persist in violating the rules, society will put them in stir and keep them there until they agree to conform. There has to be some order: drawers to put things in, hooks to hang things on, a place for everything. These are areas where everybody must be required to behave like everybody else and there is simply no escape from it. How else could we survive? To press compulsion beyond its fundamental limits, however, is to invite disaster.

Conceding the basic necessity of compulsion as we have done, the fact remains that more than this is too much. We have made education compulsory to a certain level and, no doubt, this was justifiable. How can a person survive and function creditably in our society without some minimal skills derived from his presence in school? He could do it; it has been done. But the odds against it are formidable. So much so that compulsory education is likely a sound concept. While conceding this, we must as quickly acknowledge that truly successful education cannot be coerced. Literally, one cannot force people to learn. If they don't want to, if they choose not to, they won't.

Teaching, then, becomes the art of kindling in the student a desire to learn. Many years ago I walked into a high school class in geometry, its first session of the year. I waś never any good at mathematics, cordially despised the subject, considered it an inferior discipline. The teacher, a diminutive woman with flashing brown eyes, demonstrated a proposition: "Things equal to the same thing are equal to each other." I saw it, grasped it. Then, by merest chance, she called on me to demonstrate the proposition—which I promptly and satisfactorily did.

At that point the teacher made a telling remark. I have tried many times to recall exactly what she said since this was the key to the entire episode. I think she said something like: "I see this student has a good grasp of mathematical theory." There was a faint titter from classmates who knew my limitations. But I did not titter. I have no way of explaining this, but it hit me like a bullet. I instantly made up my mind that while what the teacher said was not true, I was going to make it come true. I plunged into the geometry assignments with a dedication that would have been totally unpredictable, and I was, throughout the term, one of the top students in that class. The whole outcome was settled in one signal moment of the opening class sesson. How or why I cannot explain, but there is the fact.

Here is the secret of great teaching—and great leadership—not compelling people, but making them want to. Albert Christ-Janer, a friend for more than 40 years died in 1974. He was a great artist and a great teacher. I shall never forget visiting him one day at Pratt Institute in Brooklyn where he was the dean. I approached his classroom just as the session was concluding and the students were making their exit. I noticed a strange thing: their feet were not touching the floor! They were floating in space, their eyes a glassy stare! I gazed in utter astonishment till I realized what had happened. The teacher had literally lifted those students into another world. Class was over. They were leaving the room. Buy they had not yet returned to earth. Great teaching motivates. It kindles desire in the student so that he wills mightily to learn and will do it no matter what the odds and obstacles.

Yet even good teaching is not always enough. Sometimes, when it is great teaching, it may be enough. It may be so good that it sweeps aside every obstacle and succeeds by the sheer force of its irresistible genius. But other times—most times—even good teaching alone will not be enough. A recent survey of the Birney public school children in Washington, D.C. disclosed the disturbing fact that a third of the sixth graders could not read. This condition had apparently prevailed for years with the schools blithely passing the children on to junior high in their totally unqualified plight. On they would go to more advanced classes with their failure already an assured fact. Community rage was predictably directed at the teachers who were charged with the failure and at the superintendent who learned of the situation and ordered a halt to the promotion beyond the sixth grade of children who could not read.

The real culprits were, in all likelihood, the parents of these children. They failed to get them to bed at night because it was too much bother. They failed to provide proper food and to serve it at proper times. They failed to designate a time and place for study. They failed to ask the children what they were and were not doing at school. They failed to impose the most elementary discipline in the home. They never attended a meeting of the PTA. There was no regularity, no order, no system. The children came and went as they chose. If they went to classes, well and good. If they spent the day wandering the streets, nobody ever did anything about it. Religion and church were unheard of. In short, nobody cared. How can you solve problems like these without some system, some attention, some elementary caring in the home itself? Maybe a child can learn something by just being in school. But how much more he can learn if he has concerned adults to check him up and back him up. Education is not an automatic; education is what concerned parents and teachers make it. Their job is the most important of all—motivation.

The favorite scapegoat of our time by far is the public school. It is being blamed for everything. The churches take their licks, too, but they suffer nothing to compare with the schools. The schools must take the rap for the failures of our society. One of the most popular gambits for the politician or even the clergyman or professor is to tee off on the schools, denouncing them as hotbeds of atheism and/or communism. ("Godless atheism" is the usual expression.) All the woes and ills of mankind are heaped upon the hapless schools.

Let us reflect on this. What are the schools anyway? They are merely an extension of ourselves. They are as good as we want them to be or as bad as we let them become. The children in the classrooms are our children. The teachers are persons from our homes and churches. For the most part, the schools are not victims of outside troublemakers who have come in to create problems. The schools are the reflection of ourselves. In the long run they are what we make them.

When we are confronted with a social problem we instantly assume that its solution lies in passing some laws, setting up a government bureaucracy and expending several billion dollars of tax funds. Care of the aged offers another example. A recent book exposes the avarice of those who have seized upon this industry and exploited it for its profit-making potential. The elderly were not so much objects of their solicitude as victims of their greed. What is needed here

89

is not more laws and certainly not more expenditures of public funds, but a more intelligent use of what is presently available. It may sound simplistic, but what we really need is better, wiser leadership—a dedicated, unselfish desire to do a good job just for the sake of doing a good job.

We see the guaranteed atrophy of coercive bureaucracy in the labor movement as well. This movement has been a powerful force in our culture and still is. But it was a far more convincing force in the days when it was voluntary. People joined its ranks because they believed in it, bringing to its organization all the pristine enthusiasm of the dedicated volunteer. When membership and dues became compulsory, the structure was greatly enlarged, but the movement became less viable—in many cases a bureaucratic corpse.

The same issue confronts us in the matter of racial desegregation of the schools. Those who contend that a better education is to be had in a racially integrated school are probably correct. How to achieve it? By force, says the state, by busing necessary distances in order to surmount racial districting. Impose the program because it is good and ought to be. The result? Many whose children face a disruptive busing experience are withdrawing them from the public schools altogether and enrolling them in private schools. If the dimensions of this spread, a still more serious problem can be created. What is needed is a revival of religion that can produce changed attitudes and changed hearts. Then and only then, will all genuinely want what is good for all and welcome the sacrifice necessary to achieve it.

Then there is the problem of decent housing. All across this nation there stand gaunt reminders of government failure to solve the housing problem. These buildings are what might be called the new type slum. One looks on them in amazement. They are, at first glance, new buildings. Perhaps they were erected on the site of the vilest kind of slums that were cleared away to make room for new, handsome structures. If the needy tenants could not afford to pay the rent, again the government came to their aid with a rent supplement program. Everything was thought of; everything was done to end slums once and for all.

But as one looks more closely he begins to blink. Does he see what he seems to see? A close look at these new projects begins to exhibit many of the fatal symptoms of a slum! Perish the thought! But look again. The windows are broken. (Why do slummers always smash windows?) The doors are torn from their hinges. Trash litters the grounds. Graffiti defaces the walls. Yes, it is a slum—a brand new slum. The community has gone from slum to slum in five years because nobody cared. Let somebody finally have the nerve to say it: if those who are filthy choose to be filthy still, all the publicly (or privately) provided housing in the world will achieve nothing. When the people themselves want decent housing they can have it and it does not matter in what package it comes. The point is: people must want it, really want it, themselves!

We are concerned with the problems of trash and

litter in our cities and countryside. Somewhere the idea was born that the way to cope with the problem of litter was to impose stiff penalties. So, one constantly encounters signs announcing $100 or $50 fines for littering. Nobody ever pays the slightest attention and the trash continues to accumulate, sometimes even covering the "Don't Litter" signs. Such laws are never enforced. They could not be enforced for public opinion would not permit it. People continue to litter the streets and parks because they really like filth and prefer to live in the midst of it. When the people change their thinking and decide that they want a clean neighborhood, they can have it at once. Until they want it, they will never have it.

The grounds of the building which houses my place of employment are always spotless and clean. There is a simple explanation: the people who work there want it that way. I have seen the president and the executive director and others on the staff pause to pick up litter on the lawn and place it in a receptacle. I have done it myself many times. The result: the place is always immaculate. It is so because we want it to be so. We honestly prefer cleanliness to filth.

Voluntaryism—people wanting good things rather than evil things—people consciously and deliberately choosing what is good. How does this come about? "You must be born again," said Jesus. A whole new start is called for. You must have in you the mind of Christ so that whereas you may have once really preferred filth, you now opt for cleanliness; you once preferred ignorance or, at least, tolerated remaining in it, you now will learn; you once liked indolence and sloth, you now have a passion for honest toil. You have not a mere theoretical preference for righteousness; you embrace it with gusto. This is what you really want and you go after it with all the moral earnestness of your being. nobody is requiring it of you. nobody is forcing it on you. It is not a matter of law. It is the free, voluntary choice of your own being.

We must not be too simple about this. Getting good results does involve techniques. It does involve political and social planning. We cannot achieve good results in these areas merely by desiring them. But it is equally true that we get nowhere without desire. In the long run we shall never achieve a result, no matter how worthy, unless the people really want it.

It follows that the task of the church must be motivation. It must kindle within human beings a passion for righteousness. It must lead them to want the good and choose it. There are those who argue that the clergy should not preach politics or dabble in that area at all. They should eschew political themes and political activity. I have never felt that way. My feeling is that the clergyman has the same civil rights as others. If he wants to advance political programs, let him. He is only exercising his freedom. Besides, clergymen have advanced political ideas which are no worse than those politicians have espoused. I do not believe the clergy should be automatically barred from the political arena. There is always the chance that they might come up with something good. When that has been said, however, the fact remains that political activity represents an enormous waste of the clergyman's talent. The politician's primary concern is with technique—ways of getting things done. The clergyman's primary concern is motivation—the will to do it with whatever means are compatible with conscience. Motivation is the clergyman's concern and this lies at a deeper level. Here desire and voluntary commitment are basic. This is the realm of religion. Evangelism has always been the major concern of the churches and it remains so today. Evangelism is simply the appeal for commitment to righteousness. For the Christian it is commitment to the righteousness of Christ. When persons become Christians they become literally new persons in Christ.

To reach men and importune them with this appeal is the task of the church. It is rather pathetic to behold the clergy seeking to move in on the political scene, propounding some particular nostrum for the solution of social ills. This is not the real area of need. Social programs are a dime a dozen. Some of them are good, but none of them will ever work so long as there is no will to make them work.

During the early 1970's Church World Service was rent with dissension over its proper function in society. The organization had been set up as a united Protestant relief agency through which government could channel aid to needy peoples. It performed this service for years. But some of its leaders were not content with the program. They argued that the regimes governing these needy people were corrupt and ineffective. They ought to be changed in the best interests of the countries involved. Indeed, it was useless to keep channeling relief to nations with governments that were all wrong. Some emphasis and effort should be directed to changing the faulty regimes. The aid provided should go beyond mere relief; it should be political as well. This undoubtedly represents the thinking of many of the clergy who thus invite entanglement of church with state. If history teaches anything, it teaches that such a political program by the churches would do little for the countries they seek to serve. What is needed is a holy determination to achieve the charitable goals whatever the nature of the political regime may be.

This will to achieve is a paramount requirement for all programs. How can any program hope to succeed if people are reluctant to exert any personal effort? I participated some time ago in a TV talk show where a clergyman held forth at length on the subject of social ills. His thesis was a simple one: it was the duty of government to feed, clothe, house and provide for the entire population. Some people are interested in jobs and where these are desired government should provide them. But, regardless of this, it was government's responsibility to care for everybody.

This is a degrading credo—degrading for any government which espouses it, degrading for the persons on whom it is perpetrated. It is not the task of government to care for people save in emergency situations. It is the task of government and all properly oriented agencies to motivate people to care for themselves and to help make it possible for them to do so. This comes to something no more recondite than the old, lamented Protestant work ethic. Work is good. To work some of the time is good; much of the time is better; to work all the time is best. We can call some of our activity recreation or play if this provides comfort, but all activity should be geared to serious purpose. E.g., an hour's tennis is good, not alone because it is fun but because it helps condition one for serious work.

Max Weber has correctly and excitingly identified the constructive force in the Protestant Reformation. It was not that men were to earn their salvation. Crass presupposition! That had already been purchased for them at a price beyond comprehension. What they could and should do, however, was to "prove their calling." They could not earn their salvation, but they could demonstrate that they had been saved. Their diligence to duty would be the sure barometer of their spiritual state. This is the heart of the Protestant work ethic. To touch lives with such a kindling flame is the task of religion. While Christians share with all others a concern for good laws and capable civil administration, it is up to them to demonstrate the kind of personal dedication without which nothing can hope to succeed.

The irony of all this is that government, while it can to some extent help or hinder, cannot really do this job. Government is inextricably bound in with law and coercion. Its business, as we have seen, is the compulsory. But we have now gone far beyond the compulsory into the realm of the volitional where people are decent, clean, loving, honest, honorable and industrious because they have chosen to be so and deeply desire to be so. Motivating them in this direction is uniquely the work of religion. It is not primarily a political or social undertaking; it is a redemptive task with individuals, one by one.

The orientation of the Protestant leadership in the 1960's and 1970's almost completely ignored this basic and obvious need. The Catholic leadership has been equally at fault. The leaders have been ecumenical—making their major concern the structure of the church. It has been their objective to reduce the number of church organizations in the interest of efficiency and harmony, finally reducing them (hopefully) to one mighty and ponderous system. One could argue the merits of this proposition. Personally, I could scarcely envisage a worse disaster for the church. But the point is that all such concerns are largely irrelevant. The shape of things is of little consequence. Maybe what we need is not fewer churches, or even one great big one, but a lot more little ones. What we do need is the life-touching, life-kindling impact of religion. What we do need is something that will hit people hard, shaking them up in their sloth, making them resentful of their filth, weary of being useless, eager to be useful. In short, the people need to be converted. They must be born again. They must be motivated to righteousness in the depths of their being. If the ministries of the church have lost interest in this work or lost their capacity to perform it, where shall we turn? And if the clergy themselves protest, pleading that such an assignment is far beyond their capacity since it would require a continuous string of miracles, the answer is—precisely!

6.   A Revival of Religion

The hope of the world now, as in any age, is the hope of spiritual regeneration—that persons may be kindled and stimulated with a desire to lead effective and useful lives. This is precisely the sort of thing that invariably eludes government and never responds to coercion of any sort. And it is precisely the result that religious communities at their best have produced. Can we expect yet another resurgence from this perennially resurging sector?

The nature of the church is changing in our time. Its ecumenical thrust we have critically observed. There is an equally identifiable political thrust. The church is groping for the state, seeking government sponsorship and tax support. The trend seems to be toward a sprawling, flabby colossus with at least a quasi-official status. This trend needs prompt reversal if there is to be any hope of spiritual renewal. The church must quickly recover its function as redemptive societies of a purely voluntary character. It must resume its laborious task of redeeming persons, one by one. Government cannot do it. Coercion cannot do it. The best designed social programs cannot do it. Redemption lies in the long, hard haul of new creation. There is no other way. The task of the church is really quite simple: it must produce a million changed lives every day.

The naivete exhibited by those who seek discredited, simplistic solutions of the social problem is all but incredible. Contemplate, for example, the spectacle of those who are convinced that the gravest of problems could be solved if only enough money were transferred to the proper hands—(their own, of course). Recall the authors of the *Black Manifesto* who argued some years ago that racial injustice could be corrected if only they were given enough money. Anyone who wanted to help the cause of racial justice could do so by giving their group money. They made an initial demand for $500,000,000 in "reparations."

Money would rectify all past injustice. Money would heal all wounds, solve all problems. Money would take care of everything. Curiously, the discussion of these demands all seemed to center around their propriety. Did the establishment groups so sensationally accosted actually owe the money or not? Was it proper and just to present such demands? Apparently nobody thought to raise the question as to whether the money, if provided, would do any good.

Listen to the language of the *Manifesto:* The first task of the Internal Black Appeal is that of "raising money for the program of the National Black

Economic Development Conference." The plea continues:

> "We need money for land . . . . We must fight for massive sums of money . . . . We call for $200 million to implement this program . . . . Each of these TV networks will be funded by $10 million. The center must be funded with no less than $30 million . . . . This training center shall be funded with no less than $10 million . . . . We call for $10 million to assist in the organization of welfare recipients . . . . We call for $20 million to establish a National Black Labor Defense Fund . . . . We call for the establishment of an International Black Appeal (to be) funded with no less than $20 million- . . . . We call for the establishment of a Black University to be funded with $130 million."

The curious thing about this episode is that many religious leaders seemed to accept the reasoning of the *Black Manifesto.* They seemed to agree with the "money logic"—that if only enough money could be spent on the blacks all their problems would be solved. While little money was actually given to the International Black Appeal, many religious leaders did agree with the principle of the demands and did provide funds for more responsible black groups.

Riverside Church, New York City, where the Black Manifesto demands were first posed, referred to the program as an attempt "to exact extortion." The demands were described as "absurd and fanciful." The church did, however, pledge "a fixed percentage of its annual budget to be set apart for the rapid improvement of disadvantaged people. . . " The Executive Committee of the United Methodist Board of Missions rejected the demands of the National Black Economic Development Conference but then voted to commit $1,300,000 to its causes, the difference being that the funds would be administered by black Methodists. The United Church of Christ appeared to accept the Black Manifesto logic. The only major church which summarily rejected the Black Manifesto in principle was the Roman Catholic.

It should be observed that this acceptance of the money logic of the Black Manifesto springs from the prior acceptance of political action as the proper milieu of the church by much of the denominational leadership. This leadership has for a generation been largely committed to the proposition that the problems of mankind could be solved by good programs supported by massive government spending under the direction of the churches. When confronted with the demand that they themselves provide some massive donations; the churchmen were momentarily taken aback. But they quickly saw the point and acknowledged its force. All this accents the basic political commitment of the old-line church leadership of our time. What is the task of the church today? Certainly not the laborious business of saving souls one by one, they would argue, but rather of sponsoring and initiating social and political programs that will "save everybody"—fast.

These leaders have failed to grasp the elementary truth of the gospel that the real solution of black problems like that of white problems must come from within—through the inspired excellence of the self. It comes with the development of insights, skills, and capacities, and the assumption of disciplines. It is intimate, personal.

Top boardsmen of many major Protestant denominations, and to some extent the Roman Catholic Church as well, have, however, embraced the political emphasis. They see the work of their organizations as that of a partnership with the state in accomplishing social and political reform. They may even deny that the church has ever done anything else. Kermit Long, associate general secretary of the United Methodist Board of Evangelism, asserted that the Christian Gospel "never was personalistic and that evangelism which is not corporate and social is out of date."[1]

Dr. Long defined evangelism as a "sensitivity in the spirit of Christ to the world." He advocated a "new agenda," noting that while evangelists in former times dwelt on personal sin, the modern evangelist stresses the "guilt of man in condoning social structures that enslave people in social and spiritual ghettos" in addition to urging a turn from personal wrongdoing.

Dr. Long explained his idea of the Gospel thus:

"The Gospel calls churchmen to enter the world as it is with a readiness to hear, to respond, to suffer, serve, and love. Hearing the Gospel arouses

laymen to a brand of 'worldmanship' that deliberately seeks to alter the structures in the church, in
business and labor, in government to allow men to
be fully human and capable of responding to the
love which Christ offers."[2]

Here the Gospel is ripped from its eternal setting
and becomes a knee-jerk reaction to whatever social
gimmick happens to be in vogue at the moment.

The obsession of churchmen with materialistic
and secularist solutions of the human problem has
foundered quite as conspicuously as the Marxist effort
which was based on the same presuppositions. The
Marxists have now demonstrated that their formula
was simply inadequate. Once they have put it into
force, the Utopia they confidently expected fails to
materialize. Though they proudly achieve what they
call "social justice," they discover that the problems
and tensions of people remain about as they were.
There is still a groping for inner peace; all the problems
of personal character continue to cry out.

At this juncture the political churchman finds
himself helpless because he has already embraced the
secular solution. He, too, has focused on social justice.
He has implicitly believed that if only people were
amply furnished with secular benefits through a proper
manipulation of political forces, this would solve
everything. When he discovers that this is simply not
the case he is as baffled as the Marxist and can be of no
help to him.

John MacKay has effectively dealt with what is

really just another phase of this matter—how an exclusive concern with structure has blinded church-men to the real nature and mission of the church. The Consultation on Christian Unity has taken its assign-ment to mean the merging into a single ecclesiastical structure of several of the nation's largest denomina-tions. Here is Dr. MacKay's comment:

"The trend toward the substitution of the institutional for the communal is a flight from reality in a revolutionary and chaotic time. It ignores the serious plight in which Christian theology finds itself in many church circles today, where the reality of God is questioned, or His presence is limited to the secular order, where the new life in Christ has become largely meaningless and is disdained, where evangelism is identified with, and limited to, the effort to humanize the social environment . . . and to create a concern among those who have for those who have not. It forgets the fact that the most unified church structure in Christian history was the Roman Catholic Church in the Hispanic world. But, as is recognized in Roman Catholic circles today, this monolithic institutionalism had the most disastrous record in human annals. It created a Catholic nominalism in Latin America. It made it legitimate to say, 'I am an atheist, but I am a Catholic.' It created the most diabolic and futile clericalism in Christian history. It produced a spiritual wilder-ness. This same flight from reality, and the

105

unwillingness to wrestle with issues relating to the Eternal and the Temporal, is today producing in certain Protestant circles a mood in which institutional unity and hierarchial authority are being hailed as the one solution to all semblance of Christian dividedness.[3]

What underlies this "worldly" concept of the church is the belief that if all men were well furnished with secular benefits, then all would be well. The blunt truth which no one dares to speak is that most of the political programs espoused by the church leadership of today would probably do more harm than good. The only thing that really commends them is the fact that they are easy. There is nothing in the world easier than spending the taxpayer's money on social programs—unless it is spending the church member's donations in the same way. But whether this be done or not done, the basic task with individuals remains. It is desperately difficult—always has been so, even more so today. It is not really surprising that a new breed of churchmen has given it up altogether. To reach men with the redemptive power of the Gospel, to create a new spirit within them, one by one—and this in a day of massive over-population—no wonder the churchmen have abandoned it in favor of their pitiful nostrums! The real task of the church is one that, without God, is impossible.

Ecumenism is another concept that is totally impotent to produce a revival of religion. Its effect is not to revive but rather to embalm the church. The basic premise of ecumenism is that the Christian movement would be its best if all its diverse elements were joined in one religious organization featuring a gray consensus of beliefs which all participants could accept. Bent on such a consensus, ecumenists vie with one another in surrendering convictions to achieve it. In this quest, dedication to one's own faith is viewed as unseemly—a stone in the road of progress. Ecumencsts systematically surrender distinctive elements of their faith in order to widen their ecumenical range. The ecumenical ideal is to take in everybody and give up all convictions of individuality in belief.

There is one valid point in the ecumenical movement, and only one. Christians of the most diverse persuasions should treat each other with decency and respect. Though they may be competitive, such groups should never be hostile. They should have honest regard for each other and should always be on good speaking terms.

That, however, should be the end, not the beginning of ecumenism. The spectacle of leaders carefully assessing the temper of their company to see how much they are willing to surrender for the sake of a bland consensus is distressing, if not disgusting. This is simply not the way to a vital Christian movement. The ecumenical leaders give up everything in order to take in everybody and they end up nothing, spelled with a small "n."

Why do they do it? It is a passion for size: if only a thing is big enough it is bound to be good. It is a passion for accommodation: see what all I am willing to give up for the sake of brotherhood. It is a passion to swim in the mainstream: nobody wants to be left out. So the ecumenical experts meet and solemnly debate who will give up what to achieve a dull accommodation guaranteed to assure the apathy of all.

The pragmatic futility of the ecumenical movement should now be obvious to its most vociferous advocates. It fails to fire up anybody. It inspires no commitment. The reason, surely, is obvious: it is hard to whip up much enthusiasm for a bland consensus.

Is it mere coincidence that the non-ecumenical Mormon Church is currently the biggest gainer among major church groups? Or that Seventh-day Adventists and Jehovah's Witnesses are thriving? Consider, too, that the growing end of religion today is not in the old line (ecumenical) denominations but in a melange of sects which have never heard of the ecumenical movement and would have no interest in it if they did. It is these off-beat, narrow-gauge sects that are registering the only significant religious gains in our day. Whatever their faults and limitations, they stand for something and they demand something of their adherents. People will always respond to such an appeal.

There is a sound reason for all this. It is the unique thrust of the faith that attracts. What challenges is the appeal to take up the cross and walk a hard road. It is the sharp color that attracts the eye—not the drab gray. It is the narrowing demand that appeals—not a composite of nothings. We see this note sounded in the familiar words of Jesus: "I have not come to bring peace but a sword." Here Jesus recognizes the divisiveness of his gospel which may even divide members of the same family. Who are nearer the Gospel tradition—those who phase out differences or those who stand up for what they believe? Whatever grip the Christian Gospel may have upon men is inspired by their commitment, not by compromise and surrender.

What the professional ecumenist fails to grasp is that freedom leads inevitably to diversity. The only way to curb diversity is to curb freedom. If the COCU ecumenists have their way and achieve their super church which takes in everybody, they will do it at the expense of freedom. The suspicion is that they understand this. Do ecumenists really care about freedom? Would they prefer a spiritual monolith created and tailored by themselves?

Religious groups flourish when they concern themselves with man's need to know God in a personal relationship, and when they stress personal commitment. It does not seem to matter how bizarre and outrageous the demands, there always seem to be those who will meet them. At great cost and personal sacrifice they will take up the proffered cross in the hope that it will bring them the fulfillment they seek.

Leslie Woodson has potently capsuled the hope of Christian renewal in his *The Swinging Church:*

"Renewal of the church will come with a change in the hearts of our people who have believed that real deliverance from sin comes from

109

churchianity or that it can be found in social action. Both groups must find something deeper which will transform their attitude toward this world and their outlook for the next. The heart of renewal is the heart of a man, and whenever God can find that penitent seeker after regeneration—there the kingdom of Heaven is found and there the old enigma of sin and death is solved."[4]

Not only has the religious leadership become obsessed with politics, it has become deeply involved in commercial business. Churches have invested their surplus funds in office complexes, high rise condominiums, shopping centers, restaurants, farms and ranches, department stores, publishing houses, TV and radio stations, banks, distilleries, canneries, factories, mines, mills, and manufacturing business of various kinds. Churches are major stockholders in some of the nation's large corporations and own 10 per cent of all property in the United States. Many of these interests represent "unrelated business" since they bear no relation to the immediate concerns of religion. Because of the tax exemptions enjoyed by the churches, these ventures have proved highly lucrative. They have added substantially to the wealth and power of the religious enterprise but have done nothing for it spiritually.

This diversion to commercial business, like the absorption in ecumenism and politics, has hurt the churches. They have been led far afield from their redemptive work with persons. Indeed, when measured in terms of their historic mission, many of them seem to have lost their identity. Perhaps this helps to explain the decline of the churches which was noted in Chapter II. It would, however, be folly to write off the churches at this point. There is no regenerative potential anywhere in sight that can begin to compare with theirs. Religion has been counted out time and time again, but time and time again it has come bounding back to transform the scene. At any rate, the church is there. It exists for the redemptive purpose. It is just waiting for the revival that is long overdue.

Where can we expect this to happen? Where shall we look for it? If precedent is any guide, we must surely realize that a revival of religion is not an artifact of human creation. It is more like something that just happens, we know not how or why. Again, if precedent is any guide, the revival will not likely evolve from any of the established religious groups, nor yet from a brand new one. It will most likely come as an offshoot or dissident development from one or more of the recognized groups. Such occurrences are quite unpredictable. They are like the wind which blows as it wills. But when they happen, whatever the political system may be, lives are transformed, character is rebuilt, decency revives. There is a blessed newness of life.

Footnotes

1. *Christian Advocate*, November 28, 1968.
2. *Ibid.*
3. Bulletin of the Department of Theology of the World Alliance of Reformed Churches and the World Presbyterian Alliance, Summer 1968, Vol. VIII, Co. 4.
4. Leslie H. Woodson, *The Swinging Church—A Study in Extremes,* New York, 1970, p. 149.

Index

114